THE Film Lover's

D1041795

THE Film Lover's NEW YORK

BARBARA BOESPFLUG
BEATRICE BILLON

CHÊNE

PREFACE

This new guide contains a selection of our favorite New York addresses, offering a unique experience in connection with some of our favorite movies: you will be able to see the setting, relive the scene and feel its emotional charge, and understand what interested directors such as Martin Scorsese and Woody Allen in these fabulous places.

After Paris, New York struck us as an obvious choice: its atmosphere breathes movie-making and every street corner seems to leap straight off the screen. With passports, Metrocard© and street maps in our pockets, we set off to discover each of these legendary film locations. Of course, we were obliged to exclude the ones that had changed too much or whose owners turned us away, but our determination to enable you to relive the Big Apple on the silver screen has reaped its rewards, and we are delighted to introduce you to the film-lover's New York, accessible to all.

For ease of use, the guide is organized into neighborhoods and each entry contains practical information, including a star rating, with 1 star indicating an average price of $10, except for hotels, for which 1 star represents $100. Finally, QR codes will allow you to view trailers and film information.

We hope that the volume you hold in your hands conveys the passion that inspired us to create it in the first place.

Beatrice & Barbara

PS. The guide is based on our first-hand experience of each place, and the information included was gathered at the time of writing, during our visits and from articles and press releases, interviews, and other sources. Despite our best efforts and careful checking, it is possible that some facts will be either out of date or erroneous.

★ CONTENTS ★

UPPER WEST
& UPPER EAST SIDE

CAFE LALO

★ YOU'VE GOT MAIL ★

BY NORA EPHRON
WITH TOM HANKS, MEG RYAN
1999

 Tom Hanks discovers his virtual sweetheart

Nora Ephron knew even while she was working on the screenplay that Cafe Lalo, with its large windows and elevated position, was the right location. It had exactly the configuration she was seeking for the scene in which Tom Hanks, unable to see the girl he has a date with from the street, sends his friend to spot her from the top of the steps.

Following its appearance in the movie, the café, which opened in 1988, became one of the most popular in New York. Its Parisian bistro interior adorned with vintage posters, its delicious pastries, and its relaxing atmosphere draw a steady stream of customers throughout the day. From the outside the place is undeniably inviting, and its allure becomes even more irresistible when you see the selection of cakes, tarts, and muffins on offer. Choosing becomes harder still when you examine the menu, which includes both sweet and savory delights: the cheesecake comes in 29 flavors, the brunches draw on culinary traditions from all over the world, and the omelets can be made using various cheeses (feta, goat's cheese, cheddar, and Brie). While you wait for your order, you can enjoy a cocktail, milkshake, or coffee. For sure, you're going to have to be patient to get a table, but whether you're on a date or with friends you'll enjoy a special moment at this trendy spot.

CAFE LALO

Watch the trailer

201 W. 83rd St., NY 10024
Subway: 86th St.
☎ + 1 212-496-6031
www.cafelalo.com
Price: ★★☆☆☆

ZABAR'S

★ MANHATTAN ★

BY WOODY ALLEN
WITH WOODY ALLEN, DIANE KEATON, MICHAEL MURPHY, MARIEL HEMINGWAY, MERYL STREEP
1979

Mariel Hemingway and Woody Allen argue while shopping

Like a number of directors and actors, Woody Allen is a long-time regular customer of Zabar's and he paid homage to this loyalty in *Manhattan* by directing himself in the store with Mariel Hemingway.

Grocery store? Deli? Hardware store? Zabar's would be difficult to categorize were it not part of the lives of 35,500 New Yorkers who have been coming here every day for seventy years without stopping to ask themselves the question. With its deli section selling sandwiches to die for and tempting take-out dishes, its shelves stocked with fish and other fresh produce, its huge space devoted to cheeses from all over the world, and the famous kosher corner offering quality foodstuffs, not to mention the mezzanine devoted to kitchen utensils, you can find everything at Zabar's, which prides itself on offering high quality at low prices. The business has stayed in the family ever since it opened in 1934, and even though it occupies almost a whole block today, it has not become too big for its boots. The store is still open seven days a week, serving fresh coffee roasted on-site, another of this unusual establishment's main specialties.

ZABAR'S

Watch the trailer

2245 Broadway, NY 10024
Subway: 79th St.
☎ + 1 212-787-2000
www.zabars.com
Price: ★★☆☆☆

DAVID H. KOCH THEATER

★ BLACK SWAN ★

BY DARREN ARONOFSKY
WITH NATALIE PORTMAN, MILA KUNIS, VINCENT CASSEL, WINONA RYDER
2011

The theatre for ballet

Darren Aronofsky filmed the tortured arabesques of his black swan, Natalie Portman, on the actual stage sets of the New York City Ballet's home. He hired Frenchman Benjamin Millepied, principal dancer with the company at the time, to be the film's choreographer.

Designed by architect Philip Johnson and opened in 1964, the former New York State Theater is part of the Lincoln Center arts complex. In 2008 it was renamed after the wealthy businessman David H. Koch, who funded its renovation, which took ten years. It is the home of the New York City Ballet, the prestigious classical and modern dance company founded in 1948 by Lincoln Kirstein and George Balanchine, who were keen to create a company where young dancers could be taught by the greatest ballet masters. Today, the New York City Ballet has around one hundred dancers and performs around 150 ballets created by the likes of George Balanchine, Jerome Robbins, and Peter Martins, the company's current artistic director. The most famous stars in its history include Jacques d'Amboise, Maria Tallchief, Suki Schorer, Christopher Wheeldon, and Mikhail Baryshnikov.

DAVID H. KOCH THEATER

20 Lincoln Center Plaza, NY 10023
Subway: 66th St.
☎ + 1 212-870-5570
davidhkochtheater.com
Price: ★★★☆☆

Watch the trailer

DAKOTA BUILDING
★ ROSEMARY'S BABY ★
BY ROMAN POLANSKI
WITH MIA FARROW, JOHN CASSAVETES
1968

Home of the Woodhouse family

Built in 1884 by the architect Henry Janeway Hardenbergh, who also designed the Plaza Hotel, the Dakota Building is the oldest luxury apartment building in Manhattan, and numerous celebrities have stayed here, including Lauren Bacall, Boris Karloff, and Judy Garland. But, with its Gothic facade and towers reminiscent of a haunted manor house, it is above all the most mysterious. Ironically, it acquired gruesome notoriety around the world on the night of December 8, 1980, when John Lennon, who was a tenant there, was shot dead by a mentally disturbed man waiting for him in front of the entrance. Ever since, fans flock here every day with flowers to pay their respects, before crossing the street to bow their heads before the Strawberry Fields memorial in Central Park that is dedicated to the musician. His wife, Yoko Ono, still lives here.

Renamed the Bramford in the movie to remain faithful to the novel by Ira Levin on which it was based, the Dakota Building was chosen by Roman Polanski for its unusual and sinister look. Only the exterior of the building was filmed; the interior was recreated in the Paramount studios in Los Angeles. The building was also Tom Cruise's home at the beginning of *Vanilla Sky*.

DAKOTA BUILDING   Watch the trailer

1 W. 72nd St., NY 10023
Subway: 72nd St.
☎ + 1 212-362-1448
Price: ☆☆☆☆☆

AMERICAN MUSEUM OF NATURAL HISTORY
★ NIGHT AT THE MUSEUM ★
BY SHAWN LEVY
WITH BEN STILLER, CARLA GUGINO
2007

The museum where anything seems possible

Ever since they were kids growing up in New York, the film's two screenwriters had dreamed of being locked inside this historic American institution for the night. Although it was not possible to film inside the museum because of the risk of damaging the valuable collections, the actual facade of the building appears on screen. All the interiors were recreated in minute detail in the studio by production designer Claude Paré.

This huge natural history museum overlooking Central Park has been paying vibrant tribute to Mother Nature since 1877. The museum, whose highlights include its dinosaur displays, a replica of a huge blue whale, and the Star of India, a unique 563-carat blue sapphire, is home to nearly 32 million specimens that trace the history of the world. But its trump card is the way this wealth of exhibits is put into perspective, with visitors being led through spectacular and realistic settings. You will be kept spellbound for hours as you stroll through the 45 rooms housing the permanent displays, discovering life in the sea and on land, exploring the evolution of the earth and of animal species, and journeying through civilizations. A visit to this museum is ideal for families and is included in the CITYpass.

AMERICAN MUSEUM OF NATURAL HISTORY

Central Park West and 79th St., NY 10024-5192
Subway: 81st St.
☎ + 1 212-769-5100
www.amnh.org
Price: ★★☆☆☆

Watch the trailer

BELVEDERE CASTLE
★ 2 DAYS IN NEW YORK ★

BY JULIE DELPY
WITH JULIE DELPY, CHRIS ROCK, ALBERT DELPY, ALEXIA LANDEAU, ALEXANDRE NAHON
2012

Marion tries to save a pigeon

Belvedere Castle, designed in 1869 as a simple decorative feature to embellish the skyline, was a Victorian folly without doors or windows. It was so named because of the magnificent view it offers of Central Park. Its Neo-Gothic architecture, designed by Calvert Vaux and Jacob Wrey Mould, was inspired by a Scottish castle, and the stones used to build it were extracted from the schist on which it stands, making it look as though it has grown directly out of the ground. Thanks to its little tower, it quickly became the domain of the National Weather Center until it moved out in 1960 (a weather vane still turns atop the tower). It subsequently fell into disrepair, and was squatted and vandalized until 1983, when it was fully restored and turned into an information center for tourists, where you can obtain a fun kit for watching the park's birds.

Julie Delpy, who likes comical, absurd situations, chose to film the hilarious ending to her film in Central Park, a place she is particularly fond of. Don't worry though, the scene showing the fall was filmed against a green screen to avoid endangering the director's life, and no pigeons were harmed during filming.

BELVEDERE CASTLE

79th St., Central Park, NY 10021
Subway: 81st St.
☎ + 1 212-772-0288
www.centralparknyc.org
Price: ☆☆☆☆☆

Watch the trailer

BETHESDA FOUNTAIN
★ ENCHANTED ★

BY KEVIN LIMA
WITH AMY ADAMS, PATRICK DEMPSEY, JAMES MARSDEN, SUSAN SARANDON
2007

Princess Giselle explains her idea of true love to Robert

Even if you have never been to New York, you will probably still be familiar with the Bethesda Fountain: thanks to its romantic look, it has frequently been used in movies. Erected in 1873 in the middle of the Bethesda Terrace in Central Park, the famous statue was created by Emma Stebbins, sister of the president of the Central Park Board of Commissioners and the first woman to receive a public commission in New York City. Her work, inspired by the Gospel of John, depicts the Angel of the Waters and four cherubim representing the virtues of temperance, purity, health, and peace. Thousands of lovers stop here each year to throw in a coin and make a wish before continuing with a boat trip on the lake that it overlooks. Don't forget your camera just in case you come across a film shoot and some stars.

The Bethesda Fountain was chosen for its cherubim, which reflect the virtues of Princess Giselle, as well as for the fact that it had the requisite size for this scene, in which Central Park becomes the setting for a huge show performed by 150 stilt-walkers, gymnasts, Bavarian tap dancers, and Broadway hoofers.

BETHESDA FOUNTAIN
72nd St., Central Park, NY 10024
Subway: 72nd St.
☎ + 1 212-310-6600
www.centralparknyc.org
Price: ☆☆☆☆☆

Watch the trailer

CENTRAL PARK ZOO
★ MADAGASCAR ★

BY ERIC DARNELL & TOM MCGRATH
WITH THE VOICES OF
BEN STILLER, CHRIS ROCK, DAVID SCHWIMMER, JADA PINKETT SMITH
2005

The starting point for the story

What would our four furry friends in *Madagascar* want to escape from this lovely little haven in the middle of the city?

The little zoo in Central Park, on Fifth Avenue, provides a real breath of fresh air amid the hurly-burly of New York. Covering 6.5 hectares, it is home to nearly 130 species, and even though large animals such as the elephants, giraffes, and hippopotamuses were long ago transfered to the Bronx Zoo, it remains a delight to visit. From the Tropic zone, where birds glide about freely, to the snow leopard in his rocky lair, to the penguins that waddle around, eliciting tender smiles, this little group of animals seems to be enjoying life in their clean, well-maintained space. In particular, make sure you don't miss the sea lions being fed (11:20am, 2pm, and 4pm). For those with small children, the Tisch Children's Zoo will provide a delightful end to your visit. It has domestic animals such as small goats, cows, and lambs that are all happy to be petted. Finally, don't leave without hearing the famous chime of the magnificent clock that has become legendary following its appearance in *Madagascar*.

CENTRAL PARK ZOO   Watch the trailer

830 Fifth Ave., NY 10065
Subway: 5th Ave./59th St.
☎ + 1 212-439-6500
www.centralparkzoo.com
Price: ★☆☆☆☆

TRUMP WOLLMAN RINK
★ LOVE STORY ★

BY ARTHUR HILLER
WITH ALI MACGRAW, RYAN O'NEAL
1971

Oliver skates for Jennifer

Director Arthur Hiller had Jennifer and Oliver, as lovers do in Manhattan, go skating in a snowy Central Park for a scene of intense emotion. The film helped to make the rink famous around the world.

Ever since it opened in 1949, it has been said of the Wollman Rink that it encapsulates everything magical about New York. For lovers and families alike it is a bewitching experience to skate here, from morning to starry night, in enchanting and peaceful Central Park. New Yorkers had to wait a long time for it to reopen in 1987 after seven years of renovation work, with Donald Trump coming to the rescue by helping the city pay the bill. The rink is located a few minutes walk from the south entrance to the park, and the ice is open to all, humble beginners and seasoned skaters alike. Lessons are also available to people of all ages (kids in particular love them!). You can also watch hockey lessons and synchronized figure skating. During the summer, the ice is replaced by Victorian gardens, which are also worth visiting.

TRUMP WOLLMAN RINK

59th St. and Sixth Ave., NY 10021
Subway: 5th Ave./59th St.
☎ + 1 212-744-0882
www.wollmanskatingrink.com
Price: ★★☆☆☆

Watch the trailer

SERENDIPITY 3
★ SERENDIPITY ★

BY PETER CHELSOM
WITH JOHN CUSACK, KATE BECKINSALE
2002

Sara and Jonathan's first meeting

The first scene in the film, which illustrates perfectly the "happy accident" referred to by the word "serendipity," was actually filmed on the second floor of the famous Manhattan restaurant, but due to time constraints the director had to film the second scene on a set that was a meticulous recreation in the studios in Toronto.

Opened in 1954, the legendary Serendipity 3 was named after a story by the English writer Horace Walpole, in which three princes of Serendip were regarded as heroes because of their extraordinary chance discoveries. Its incredible decor is like something out of a fairy tale, filled with knick-knacks, chandeliers, and tableware that seem to come straight out of *Alice in Wonderland*. But the desserts are what make this restaurant one of the most memorable in Manhattan. These include Frrrozen Hot Chocolate, which has beguiled many a celebrity, from Marilyn Monroe, who for this dessert alone made this her favorite place in New York, to Andy Warhol, who, although unknown at the time, paid his bill with artwork, to Jackie Kennedy Onassis, who wanted to buy the recipe, but was only allowed to watch it being made.

SERENDIPITY 3

225 E. 60th St., NY 10022
Subway: Lexington Ave./59th St.
☎ + 1 212-838-3531
www.serendipity3.com
Price: ★★☆☆☆

Watch the trailer

ROOSEVELT ISLAND AERIAL TRAM
★ LÉON ★

BY LUC BESSON
WITH NATALIE PORTMAN, JEAN RENO, GARY OLDMAN
1994

🎥 *Mathilda goes back to school*

In the final scene of the movie, Luc Besson shows Natalie Portman traveling above Manhattan aboard a cable car, as if to symbolize that she is leaving a life of crime behind and returning to a more conventional one—that of an adolescent returning to school.

When the hustle and bustle of Manhattan becomes too oppressive, many New Yorkers take this odd aerial tram to Roosevelt Island for a picnic on the grass, away from the noise of the city. More ecological than a helicopter and largely unknown to tourists, the trip is enough to make you dizzy. Costing no more than the price of a subway ticket, the ride in the cabin more than 250 feet above the water is thrilling, with a stunning view, especially at sunrise or sunset, of Manhattan, Queens, and the East River. Built in 1976 by the Swiss company Von Roll, the Roosevelt Island Tramway was initially intended to be a temporary solution before the opening in 1989 of the F subway line serving the island. Thanks to its popularity with locals, it became a permanent facility. In 2010, it was renovated by the French company Poma. More than 26 million travelers have used it since it was built nearly forty years ago.

ROOSEVELT ISLAND AERIAL TRAM   Watch the trailer

59th St. and Second Ave., NY 10022
Subway: Lexington Ave./59th St.
☎ + 1 212-832-4555
www.rioc.com
Price: ★☆☆☆☆

J.G. MELON
★ KRAMER VS. KRAMER ★

BY ROBERT BENTON
WITH MERYL STREEP, DUSTIN HOFFMAN, JUSTIN HENRY
1980

Joanna and Ted Kramer fight over custody of their child

In order to surprise Meryl Streep, Dustin Hoffman told no one but the cameraman that he was going to hurl his wine glass at the wall. The actress's shocked reaction is thus authentic, but Streep waited until the director called "cut" before having a word with Hoffman about it.

In 1972, Jack O'Neill and George Mourge—the "J" and the "G" in J.G. Melon—opened a restaurant in an Irish pub. The wood-paneled decor and quiet ambience were kept, while improbable photos and paintings of watermelons were added. The menu consists of American fare, including the restaurant's trademark burger, served with crisp round French fries or a green salad. The meat, juicy and tasty, is simply garnished with lettuce, a slice of tomato, onion, and pickle. This burger, unquestionably one of the finest in the city, rapidly turned J.G. Melon into an Upper East Side institution, frequented by politicians, artists, and even the Kennedy family. Today, the dining room is always full and you need to be patient to get a table. Those in a hurry can always enjoy a quick bite at the bar. A word of warning: credit cards are not accepted, so make sure you have cash.

J.G. MELON

1291 Third Ave., NY 10021
Subway: 77th St.
☎ + 1 212-744-0585
Price: ★★☆☆☆

Watch the trailer

SANT AMBROEUS
★ W.E. ★

BY MADONNA
WITH ABBIE CORNISH, ANDREA RISEBOROUGH, JAMES D'ARCY, OSCAR ISAAC
2012

 Tête-à-tête between Wally and Evgeni

This fashionable Manhattan Italian restaurant had all the ingredients Madonna was looking for as a location in her movie.

Opened in 1982 by the Pauli family, the restaurant, a popular hangout for locals, as well as numerous celebrities such as Bono, Lenny Kravitz, Harrison Ford, and Matt Dillon, is a perfect marriage of the Milanese tradition with current trends. When you bear the name of the patron saint of Milan, you are duty-bound to offer wholesome Italian dishes: for breakfast, espressos and cappuccinos are accompanied by irresistible Italian pastries, while the other meals of the day include such specialties as a divine risotto and a *cotoletta alla Milanese* to die for, as well as panini that are a boon for customers in a hurry. Here it would be sacrilege to spurn the desserts, but between the Pumpkin Cheese Cake, which remains on the menu long after Thanksgiving, and the delicious Chocolate Mousse, it's an agonizing choice. Finally, to the delight of those with palates accustomed to excellence, the wine list consists of a judicious selection of the finest nectars of the Italian gods.

SANT AMBROEUS MADISON

1000 Madison Ave., NY 10075
Subway: 77th St.
☎ + 1 212-570-2211
www.santambroeus.com
Price: ★★★☆☆

Watch the trailer

LEXINGTON CANDY SHOP
★ THREE DAYS OF THE CONDOR ★

BY SYDNEY POLLACK
WITH ROBERT REDFORD, FAYE DUNAWAY
1975

Robert Redford comes to order the team's lunch

The Lexington Candy Shop, located three blocks from the Metropolitan Museum of Art, was opened in 1925 and renovated in 1948. Since then, it has not aged at all. In the fantastic retro interior of this superb luncheonette, customers revel in the atmosphere of a 1950s diner. It offers friendly, old-style service from staff clad in white chef's jackets or aprons, in keeping with a tradition that has been upheld for three generations by the Philis family.

Open seven days a week, the Candy Shop makes all sorts of sweets and drinks such as sundaes, sodas, and milkshakes, and serves diner food that is freshly prepared each morning. Their pancakes, burgers, cheddar cheese omelets, and sandwiches are guaranteed to torpedo any diet resolutions, although those with smaller appetites will be delighted by the selection of salads on the menu. By way of a sweet, and despite the restaurant's name, we recommend sampling the house ice cream of the month.

In Sydney Pollack's movie, the Candy Shop plays its real-life role of neighborhood spot frequented by regulars. They include Robert Redford, who comes from his office nearby to order something.

LEXINGTON CANDY SHOP   Watch the trailer

1226 Lexington Ave., NY 10028
Subway: Lexington Ave./86th St.
☎ + 1 212-288-0057
www.lexingtoncandyshop.net
Price: ★★☆☆☆

MIDTOWN

THE PLAZA
★ THE GREAT GATSBY ★

BY BAZ LUHRMANN
WITH LEONARDO DICAPRIO, TOBEY MAGUIRE, CAREY MULLIGAN, ISLA FISHER
2013

Grandeur and decadence in muggy New York

To remain faithful to the novel by F. Scott Fitzgerald, a regular notorious for his escapades at The Plaza, the film version of *Gatsby* had to feature the hotel. Production designer Catherine Martin, who had previously won two Oscars for her work on *Moulin Rouge*, did a lot of research in the hotel's archives to ensure that the 1920s atmosphere, and in particular the lighting, would be accurately recreated in the studio. For the outdoor scenes, the real building was digitally inserted into a period setting.

The Plaza is one of the most famous hotels in America, and ever since it was built it has lived up to its motto, "Nothing unimportant ever happens at The Plaza." Bernhard Beinecke, Fred Sterry, and Harry S. Black had the crazy dream of building this nineteen-story edifice in New York's smartest neighborhood, a project that took two years and cost twelve million dollars—an astronomical sum at the time. The decoration of this building, designed in the style of a French chateau, is sumptuous throughout. For more than one hundred years, the establishment has been frequented by the world's most important people, including legendary artists such as the novelist and his wife, for whom it was almost a second home.

THE PLAZA   Watch the trailer
768 Fifth Ave., NY 10019
Subway: 5th Ave./59th St.
☎ + 1 212-759-3000
www.fairmont.com/the-plaza-new-york
Price: ★ ★ ★ ★ ★

FAO SCHWARZ
★ BIG ★

BY PENNY MARSHALL
WITH TOM HANKS, ELIZABETH PERKINS
1988

Tom Hanks takes on the giant piano

For over one hundred and fifty years, FAO Schwarz has had only one vocation: to fill young and old alike with wonder. Located on prestigious Fifth Avenue, the store looks like Father Christmas's secret stash, where alluring toys of every kind rub shoulders, from the latest trends to traditional wooden toys. Lego sets, Barbies, Hello Kitties, dinosaurs, Uglydolls, toy soldiers, interactive dolls, and soft toys from all over the world are arranged into their respective worlds across two huge floors. And watch out for the sugar rush on the first floor, which is overflowing with mountains of irresistible candy. Although it is now owned by the giant Toys"R"Us, the store has lost none of its opulence and remains a temple of fun. It is at its most resplendent in December, when its fabulous Christmas windows never fail to enchant.

FAO Schwarz played an important role in the movie *Big*, in which Tom Hanks, as a child in an adult's body, played the keys of the giant floor piano. Ever since this legendary scene, the store has been a popular attraction in New York, with hordes of children flocking here every day to run amok.

FAO SCHWARZ
767 Fifth Ave., NY 10022
Subway: 5th Ave./59th St.
☎ + 1 212-644-9400
www.fao.com
Price: ★★★☆☆

Watch the trailer

TIFFANY & CO.
★ BREAKFAST AT TIFFANY'S ★

BY BLAKE EDWARDS
WITH AUDREY HEPBURN, GEORGE PEPPARD, PATRICIA NEAL
1962

Audrey Hepburn eats breakfast in front of Tiffany & Co.

In keeping with Truman Capote's story, Blake Edwards filmed Audrey Hepburn at Tiffany's, which agreed to make an exception and open on a Sunday. Twenty security guards were assigned to watch over the millions of dollars worth of jewelry on display amid the film crew. Nothing was stolen!

Opened in 1940, the Tiffany & Co. store on Fifth Avenue is the brand's most famous outlet, one whose history encapsulates the American dream. It all began in 1837, when Charles L. Tiffany and John Young, with only one thousand dollars in their pockets, opened a store selling silver stationery items in Lower Manhattan. Following its success, they shifted their focus to gold jewelry. But it was the fall in the price of diamonds in the late 19th century that provided them with a real opportunity: it enabled them to acquire diamonds from wealthy people fallen on hard times and to use these precious gemstones to make jewelry. Their talent for exhibiting their creations at the various world's fairs marked Tiffany's entrance into the select circle of great jewelers, paving the way for the store on famous Fifth Avenue.

Even if you can't afford to buy one of the solitaires in the window, you should at least go upstairs to admire the largest yellow diamond in the world, which weighs a dizzying 128 carats.

TIFFANY & CO.

Fifth Ave. and 57th St., NY 10022
Subway: 5th Ave./59th St.
☎ + 1 212-755-8000
www.tiffany.com
Price: ★★★★☆

Watch the trailer

ST. REGIS HOTEL
★ TAXI DRIVER ★

BY MARTIN SCORSESE
WITH ROBERT DE NIRO, JODIE FOSTER, HARVEY KEITEL, CYBILL SHEPHERD
1976

 Betsy leaves the hotel to take a taxi

At a time when New York was a city with one of the highest crime rates in the world, the St. Regis reflected perfectly the status of Betsy, a campaign worker for the senator.

Built by one of the richest men in America, John Jacob Astor IV, who went down with the *Titanic*, the St. Regis opened its sumptuous doors in 1904. With its unrivaled luxury and level of service, and its butlers on-call round the clock, the hotel remains one of the most expensive places in New York. Even if you don't stay here, the carved ceilings, crystal chandeliers, and Louis XVI furniture are all worth seeing.

ST. REGIS HOTEL   Watch the trailer

2 E. 55th St., NY 10022
Subway: 5th Ave./53rd St.
☎ + 1 212-753-4500
www.stregisnewyork.com
Price: ★★★★★

SUBWAY GRATE
★ THE SEVEN YEAR ITCH ★

BY BILLY WILDER
WITH MARILYN MONROE, TOM EWELL
1955

 Richard is enjoying a stroll with his neighbor when her dress billows up

This scene, one of the most famous in film history, was the idea of Sam Shaw, a friend of Marilyn's, who had previously photographed a group of girls, one with her dress billowing up in a gust of air. Numerous excited onlookers had gathered to see the star and her underwear on Lexington Avenue, which was closed for the occasion. The noise made by the crowd forced the director to ask the star to redo the scene several times, before he eventually gave in and agreed to shoot it in the studio. These few minutes also ended Marilyn's marriage to Joe DiMaggio, who was furious to see his wife exhibiting herself in this way in front of so many men.

SUBWAY GRATE   Watch the trailer

Corner of 52th St. and Lexington Ave., NY
Subway: Lexington Ave./53th St.

WALDORF ASTORIA
★ WEEK-END AT THE WALDORF ★

BY ROBERT Z. LEONARD
WITH GINGER ROGERS, LANA TURNER, WALTER PIDGEON, VAN JOHNSON
1947

Backdrop to a film

The Waldorf serves as the basis for the film's storyline, which centers around the lives of the hotel's guests and staff. Although only a few scenes were actually shot there, an exhibition in the lobby pays tribute to the movie.

Located at its current address since 1931, after having moved a few blocks following the Wall Street Crash of 1929, the Waldorf Astoria, with its 47 floors, is still one of the tallest Art Deco buildings in the world. Its architecture has led it to be listed by the National Trust for Historic Preservation. Luxurious in every way, this is one of the most celebrated grand hotels in the world. Its excellence is evident from the moment you enter the lobby, which is open to everyone. The establishment is also unique in being split into two parts: the 1st to 26th floors are occupied by a traditional hotel, while the 27th to 42nd are taken up by the select Waldorf Towers, luxury apartments with their own private entrance. Another unusual feature is found underneath the hotel: a train platform leading to Grand Central that was secretly used by President Franklin D. Roosevelt when he visited the city, and by Andy Warhol when he threw his Underground Party.

WALDORF ASTORIA

301 Park Ave., NY 10022
Subway: Lexington Ave./51st St.
☎ + 1 212-355-3000
www.waldorfastoria3.hilton.com
Price: ★★★★☆

Watch the trailer

THE ROOSEVELT HOTEL
★ MAN ON A LEDGE ★
BY ASGER LETH
WITH SAM WORTHINGTON, ELIZABETH BANKS
2012

Sam Worthington goes out on the ledge

Opened in 1924, when the Jazz Age was in full swing, the Roosevelt Hotel, named in honor of the president and known as "the Grand Dame of Madison Avenue," has lost none of its original splendor. Its large lobby, a monument to the elegance of the Roaring Twenties, harks back to the grandeur of old New York. The 1995 make-over and the high-tech features in its 1,015 rooms, including 52 suites, have in no way impaired the old-fashioned atmosphere wafting around the floors. As well as boasting a classic restaurant (the Roosevelt Grill), an old school bar (the Madison Club Lounge), an after-work bar (the Vander Bar), and a rooftop terrace lounge with a postcard view (mad46), the hotel also has a fully-equipped business center for business travelers. The Roosevelt is located a few blocks from Rockefeller Center, Grand Central, and Times Square, and the divine beds are a boon for backs aching from marathon shopping expeditions.

The movie's production designer recreated an exact replica of the 21st-story room on the roof to make it easier to create the dizzying shots of the actor standing on the ledge—quite an achievement for Sam Worthington, who has always suffered from vertigo.

THE ROOSEVELT HOTEL   Watch the trailer

45 E. 45th St. and Madison Ave., NY 10017
Subway: Grand Central
☎ + 1 212-661-9600
www.theroosevelthotel.com
Price: ★★★☆☆

GRAND CENTRAL TERMINAL
★ REVOLUTIONARY ROAD ★

BY SAM MENDES
WITH KATE WINSLET, LEONARDO DICAPRIO, MICHAEL SHANNON, KATHY BATES
2009

Frank arrives in the city

Located in the heart of Manhattan, Grand Central Terminal, with its 60 tracks, its subway station, its 30 or so dining options, its fresh-food market and the numerous stores in the passages, is the largest station in the world. Opened in 1913, Grand Central has just celebrated its centennial, which it came close to never reaching. In the 1970s rail travel was facing growing competition from airlines, and the building, which was dilapidated and frequented by drug dealers, was almost torn down. Fortunately, thanks in part to the support of Jackie Kennedy Onassis, who was shocked at the prospect of this superb Beaux-Arts edifice disappearing, it was saved and transformed into a commuter hub. Often used by the film industry, it is today a must-visit destination for tourists, who marvel at the Main Concourse, its ceiling painted with 2,500 stars by Paul-César Helleu, and its legendary clock, located in the middle, above the information desks.

In the film, the hero, played by Leonardo DiCaprio, is shown traveling into Manhattan from the suburbs. For cost reasons, it was only possible for the station to be closed for part of the day. The way it was shot, the interior dark and dull, was partly inspired by a book of photographs by Saul Leiter.

GRAND CENTRAL TERMINAL   Watch the trailer

87 E. 42nd St., NY 10017
Subway: Grand Central
www.grandcentralterminal.com
Price: ☆☆☆☆☆

PERSHING SQUARE
★ THE AVENGERS ★

BY JOSS WHEDON
WITH ROBERT DOWNEY JR., CHRIS EVANS, MARK RUFFALO, CHRIS HEMSWORTH,
SCARLETT JOHANSSON, JEREMY RENNER
2012

Unknown evil forces are attacking New York

Symbols of the hustle and bustle of New York, Pershing Square and 42nd Street serve as a battleground for the Avengers© in a destructive clash with the forces of evil. Although the on-screen illusion is perfect, the scene was actually shot on East 9th Street in downtown Cleveland.

At first glance, the long Pershing Square restaurant, tucked under the viaduct leading to Grand Central Terminal, might look like a run-of-the-mill place where people come while waiting for their train. The impression is misleading, however. If you enter the red neon facade you'll be surprised to discover an elegant, old-fashioned decor. Once inside, you will be shown to one of the booths that run the length of the huge windows, or else to one of the central tables beneath the green iron railroad beams. We particularly recommend the breakfast, said to be one of the best in town, not least because of the pancakes. But the lunch and dinner menus, popular with businesspeople and families alike, are also above reproach: the Signature Chicken Pot Pie and the House Made Ricotta Ravioli, brought by smartly dressed wait staff, add to the magic of this one-of-a-kind establishment.

PERSHING SQUARE   Watch the trailer

90 E. 42nd St., NY 10017
Subway: Grand Central/42nd St.
☎ + 1 212-286-9600
www.pershingsquare.com
Price: ★★★☆☆

THE NEW YORK PUBLIC LIBRARY
★ THE DAY AFTER TOMORROW ★

BY ROLAND EMMERICH
WITH DENNIS QUAID, JAKE GYLLENHAAL
2004

The survivors' refuge

With its powerful architecture and image as custodian of the written documents of American history, the New York Public Library has often appeared in films, serving as an indestructible refuge for the hero. It appears, for example, in *Spider-Man 1*, *Spider-Man 3*, *Ghostbusters*, and *Escape from New York*.

Although the NYPL has several libraries scattered around the city, it is best known for the large edifice that has stood on Fifth Avenue since 1911. Designed by the architectural firm of Carrère and Hastings, the building appears to be guarded by two huge lions sculpted by Edward Clark Potter. Originally called Leo Astor and Leo Lenox, they were renamed Fortitude and Patience in 1930 by Fiorello LaGuardia, who was the city's mayor at the time. These nicknames are not inappropriate, for both courage and time are required to explore the library's fifty million books and documents, which can be consulted by anyone, free of charge. And even if you do not feel like reading, you are still welcome to go in and explore the maze of corridors and stone staircases, and the majestic main reading room where the rows of absorbed readers extend for 297 feet under the 52-foot high ceilings.

THE NEW YORK PUBLIC LIBRARY Watch the trailer

476 Fifth Ave., NY 10018
Subway: Grand Central
☎ + 1 917-275-6975
www.nypl.org
Price: ☆☆☆☆☆

SARDI'S
★ THE MUPPETS TAKE MANHATTAN ★
BY FRANK OZ
WITH LIZA MINNELLI, DABNEY COLEMAN, JOHN LANDIS, ELLIOTT GOULD
1984

 *Kermit appears at Sardi's*

In this hilarious scene, director Frank Oz immortalized the restaurant's real owner, Vincent Sardi Jr., in the company of a famous customer, Liza Minnelli, who flies into a rage when she sees that her caricature is no longer on the wall.

When you eat at Sardi's you get to see the history of Broadway. The restaurant opened at its present address, in the heart of the Theater District, in 1927. In order to attract celebrities who were performing in the neighborhood, it cleverly pinched an original concept from Joe Zelli's, a fashionable Parisian jazz club, by hiring a caricaturist who would poke fun at customers in caricatures that would then be displayed on the walls. The first artist to wield his pencils was Alex Gard, a Russian refugee who, up until his death in 1948, produced around 700 works, which were paid for in meals. Success was virtually immediate and leading figures from the art world happy to be sent up flocked here to be immortalized. The tradition has continued, and there are now more than 1,300 portraits on display in the restaurant. The tasty dishes on offer, such as Spinach Cannelloni Au Gratin, have also contributed to its excellent reputation.

SARDI'S RESTAURANT AND GRILL   Watch the trailer

234 W. 44th St., NY 10036
Subway: Times Sq.
☎ + 1 212-221-8440
www.sardis.com
Price: ★★★☆☆

SARDI'S
PARK
PARK
Discovery
TIMES SQUARE
POMPEII
THE
EXHIBIT
RESTAURANT
COCKTAILS

The caricatures on the walls poke fun at customers.

HOTEL EDISON
★ THE GODFATHER ★

BY FRANCIS FORD COPPOLA
WITH MARLON BRANDO, AL PACINO, JAMES CAAN, ROBERT DUVALL, DIANE KEATON
1972

🎥 *The killing of Luca Brasi*

Francis Ford Coppola filmed in the long corridor that leads to the superb lobby, which can also be seen in Woody Allen's *Bullets over Broadway*. The scene then continues in the hotel's legendary Sofia restaurant, which is sadly no longer open.

The Hotel Edison is located in the heart of the Theater District, blending right in with its neighbors. Its Art Deco facade, unchanged since it was built in 1931, fills almost an entire city block. Designed in a similar style to the Radio City Music Hall, it is perfectly at home amid the bright lights of Broadway. Not surprisingly, its huge ballroom, which became famous as a venue for the some of the greatest names in jazz, became a theater between 1950 and 1991, before returning to its Swing Era vocation of making people dance. The rest of the hotel is in step with the period feel, notably the frescoes in the lobby, which have lost none of their charm. Check out the adjoining Café Edison, which is popular with Midtown workers and theater-goers just before show time. It, too, has conserved its original aura.

EDISON HOTEL　Watch the trailer

228 W. 47nd St., NY 10036
Subway: 49th St./7th Ave.
☎ + 1 212-840-5000
www.edisonhotelnyc.com
Price: ★★★★☆

ELLEN'S STARDUST DINER
★ NEW YEAR'S EVE ★

BY GARRY MARSHALL
WITH ROBERT DE NIRO, ASHTON KUTCHER, ZAC EFRON, SARAH JESSICA PARKER, MICHELLE PFEIFFER
2011

Sarah Jessica Parker finds her daughter in Times Square

For over a century now, the ball drop from the top of One Times Square in New York has been one of the main festivities marking the beginning of the New Year. It takes place next door to a famous neighbor, Ellen's Stardust Diner, another pillar of American tradition, which just had to feature in the film for the picture to be complete.

Those who have small appetites or who love peace and quiet should steer clear of this place, for Ellen's Stardust pulls no punches, offering lavish dishes and high-spirited service. Indeed, the restaurant is unique in Manhattan in that its essentially simple cuisine, in which burgers and French fries washed down with milkshakes take center stage, is served by budding actors and singers, who belt out numbers as if they were in a musical. And because the American standards they launch into are familiar to all, diners happily join in the chorus between mouthfuls. When "New York New York" comes round, it's pretty much impossible to resist singing along. Of course, the diner's decor reflects its "Grease" ambience, and because of its location on Times Square, the place is mostly frequented by tourists. All the more reason to cast aside your inhibitions and set your vocal chords free!

ELLEN'S STARDUST DINER   Watch the trailer

1650 Broadway, NY 10019
Subway: 50th St.
☎ + 1 212-956-5151
www.ellensstardustdiner.com
Price: ★★☆☆☆

21 CLUB

★ WALL STREET ★

BY OLIVER STONE
WITH MICHAEL DOUGLAS, MARTIN SHEEN, CHARLIE SHEEN, DARYL HANNAH
1988

 Bud Fox is invited to the 21 Club for a steak tartare

In choosing the 21 Club, Oliver Stone was situating the action at one of the city's most symbolic addresses, a place where business is conducted. *Forbes* claimed in 1980 that "more deals are done at '21' than on the stock market floor."

Opened during Prohibition, the Club 21 earned its reputation in part thanks to New York mayor Jimmy Walker, who would come here secretly for a drink at a time when it was an illegal speakeasy. The place quickly acquired an exclusive aura, becoming popular with men born to wealthy families who were drawn by the thrill of the illicit. Mementoes of some of these families can be seen outside in the row of cast-iron jockeys honoring the leading stables of thoroughbred racing in the country. Although absolutely anyone can dine here, jeans and sneakers are forbidden (ties are now no longer compulsory though). Smart dress is de rigueur in this elegant restaurant, where just about every U.S. president has dined. Dishes such as caviar, lobster, the Seafood Tower, chicken a la plancha, and the "21" burger fit perfectly with this VIP ambience.

21 CLUB   Watch the trailer

21 W. 52nd St., NY 10019
Subway: 5th Ave./53rd St.
☎+1 212-582-7200
www.21club.com
Price: ★★★★☆

CARNEGIE DELI
★ BROADWAY DANNY ROSE ★

BY WOODY ALLEN
WITH WOODY ALLEN, MIA FARROW, NICK APOLLO FORTE, JACKIE GAYLE
1984

 The opening scene of the film

The Carnegie Deli should get official recognition for its services to the public good such is the quality of its cold cuts, which are salt-cured and smoked in its own plant. Ever since it opened in 1937, customers have been flocking here by the thousands—including numerous celebrities—to try its famous pastrami sandwich, which is filled with over a pound of meat. Even though this modest deli has tripled in size since the early days, you still often have to wait to get a table or order take-out. As a mark of his fondness for the place, Woody Allen chose this deli as a setting for several scenes in *Broadway Danny Rose*, and ever since there has been a sandwich on the menu that bears the director's name.

CARNEGIE DELI
854 Seventh Ave., NY 10019
Subway: 7th Ave.
☎ + 1 212-757-2245
www.carnegiedeli.com
Price: ★★☆☆☆

Watch the trailer

THE RUSSIAN TEA ROOM
★ TOOTSIE ★

BY SYDNEY POLLACK
WITH DUSTIN HOFFMAN, JESSICA LANGE, TERI GARR, BILL MURRAY
1983

 Tootsie listens, stunned, to all the nasty things her agent is saying about her

Ever since it was created in 1927 by members of the Imperial Russian Ballet, the Russian Tea Room has been elegantly hosting the intellectual and artistic elite, in particular famous actors, writers, and leading political figures, often after a show at nearby Carnegie Hall. They come here for the refined cuisine, a delicate cup of tea, or a rare vodka. While soaking up the plush, distinguished decor, in which the power of Great Russia hovers over the soft lighting of the tables, make sure you remember to seek out the coat check, where Louise Ciccone worked before becoming Madonna, and the table where Dustin Hoffman sat dressed as Tootsie.

THE RUSSIAN TEA ROOM

150 W. 57th St., NY 10019
Subway: 7th Ave.
☎ + 1 212-581-7100
www.russiantearoomnyc.com
Price: ★★★★☆

Watch the trailer

CHELSEA
& UNION SQUARE

THE GOLF CLUB AT CHELSEA PIERS
★ THE OTHER GUYS ★

BY ADAM MCKAY
WITH MARK WAHLBERG, WILL FERRELL, SAMUEL L. JACKSON, DWAYNE JOHNSON, EVA MENDES
2010

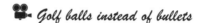 *Golf balls instead of bullets*

Want to play golf in New York? No problem! The club at Chelsea Piers has three simulators that give you the chance to "play" on one of fifty courses carefully chosen from the best in the world. What's even more enjoyable is to drive some balls outside from one of the hitting stalls arranged on four levels overlooking the Hudson. The amazing green may be surrounded by a high fence, but it is still fun to try to hit the ball all the way into New Jersey. The club is aware of the importance of creating the right atmosphere for a sport that is popular above all for its outdoor aspect. There is a green for you to practice your putting, where the décor enables you to forget about the soulless hangar housing it. Lessons with former pros for players of all levels can also be booked, and all the equipment you need is available for rental. Lastly, in keeping with tradition, there is a welcoming clubhouse, offering a selection of beers and whiskies, together with some refreshing snacks, where players can discuss the finer points of their golf swing at the end of a session. Around 20 movies have used this incredible setting, including *The Other Guys*, which had a helicopter explode in the middle of the course.

THE GOLF CLUB AT CHELSEA PIERS   Watch the trailer

Pier 59, Chelsea Piers, NY 10011
Subway: 23rd St.
☎ + 1 212-336-6400
www.chelseapiers.com
Price: ★★★☆☆

THE HIGH LINE
★ SIDE EFFECTS ★

BY STEVEN SODERBERGH
WITH ROONEY MARA, CHANNING TATUM, JUDE LAW, CATHERINE ZETA-JONES
2013

🎥 *Emily and Martin's happier times*

Steven Soderbergh wanted to film on location in order to give his movie an authentic New York atmosphere and to make his scenes as realistic as possible. He also likes places that are unusual or that have not appeared in movies before, such as the High Line.

This superb green walk, situated 30 feet above the streets of Manhattan's West Side, is the product of a remarkable campaign fought by a number of people. It was built as a freight line, but fell into decline in the 1950s with the rise of road haulage; the last train ran in 1980. With the tracks abandoned, the owners of the land underneath, together with Rudolph Giuliani, then mayor of New York, called for its destruction. But in 1999 some local residents founded the Friends of the High Line association to campaign for its transformation into a "park in the sky." They succeeded in getting the support of new mayor Michael Bloomberg, who allocated $50 million in public funds to the project, which was inspired by the Promenade Plantée in Paris's 12th *arrondissement*. Since opening in 2009, it has given Lower Manhattan a new lung. On sunny days, the 23rd Street Lawn is permanently packed.

THE HIGH LINE   Watch the trailer

23rd St., NY 10011
Subway: 23rd St.
☎ + 1 212-500-6035
www.thehighline.org
Price: ☆☆☆☆☆

THE HALF KING
★ GOING THE DISTANCE ★
BY NANETTE BURSTEIN
WITH DREW BARRYMORE, JUSTIN LONG, CHRISTINA APPLEGATE
2010

Erin and Garrett fall in love

Although it was not written into the original script, the director nevertheless wanted to show the burgeoning love between her two characters. The beginning of this scene, which opens in a diner, was filmed on a Saturday evening at the Half King, with a hand-held camera for added realism.

Since it opened in 2000, the Half King, named after an Iroquois chief, has been something of a rebel compared with the more traditional restaurants in the neighborhood. This may be partly due to the co-owner, Sebastian Junger, war correspondent and author of the book *The Perfect Storm*, which was made into the film of the same name, and partly due to the menu devised by chef Gregory Baumel, which aims to provide copious meals, of a quality worthy of the finest establishments, and at affordable prices. Whether you come for the burger boxes, which include the extraordinary Tuna Quinoa, or for its Macaroni and Cheese—without a doubt the best in New York—or for the weekend brunch, this relaxed saloon has a lot going for it, including a small garden where you can enjoy a drink when the weather permits. Finally, in keeping with the restaurant's aim of offering people a tasty meal or a beer while stimulating the intellect, literary events are held each week.

THE HALF KING BAR & RESTAURANT

505 W. 23rd St., NY 10011
Subway: 23rd St.
☎ + 1 212-462-4300
www.thehalfking.com
Price: ★★☆☆☆

Watch the trailer

CHELSEA HOTEL
★ 9¹ᐟ² WEEKS ★

BY ADRIAN LYNE
WITH KIM BASINGER, MICKEY ROURKE, MARGARET WHITTON
1986

One fantasy too many for John

With its 12-story red-brick Gothic facade, the Chelsea Hotel is as legendary as the personalities who have lived there. Built in 1883, the building became a hotel in 1905, with its location in the middle of the theater district bringing it a new bohemian clientele. And when Stanley Bard, its owner from 1955 to 2007, began offering penniless artists a roof, he created an extraordinary crucible where major works and events of 20th-century underground culture were created: Kerouac wrote *On the Road* there, Arthur C. Clarke worked on his *2001, A Space Odyssey* there while Kubrick, also a resident at one point, was developing the film version, and Mark Twain, Arthur Miller, Tennessee Williams, Dennis Hopper, Jane Fonda, Andy Warhol, Jimi Hendrix, Leonard Cohen, Bob Dylan, and Patti Smith also lived there. More tragically, Sid Vicious contributed to the Chelsea's renown by killing his girlfriend Nancy in his room.

Since it was bought in 2011 by a businessman whose exact plans remain unclear, the place has been closed for renovation, except to the one hundred or so permanent residents who want to stay put despite the difficult living conditions. But for how long?

CHELSEA HOTEL
222 W. 23rd St., NY 10011
Subway: 23rd St.
☎ + 1 646-918-8770
www.hotelchelsea.com

Watch the trailer

EMPIRE STATE BUILDING
★ KING KONG ★

BY ERNEST B. SCHOEDSACK & MERIAN C. COOPER
WITH FAY WRAY, ROBERT ARMSTRONG, BRUCE CABOT
1933

King Kong confronts his attackers

When *King Kong* was made in 1933, the skyscraper, completed two years before, was the pride of America, the tallest building in the world. For the screenwriters, it was the only building that could match up to the huge gorilla.

A symbol of New York, this monument to Art Deco borrows the state's nickname: "The Empire State." Regarded as one of the seven wonders of the modern world by the American Society of Civil Engineers, the building lords over Midtown on Fifth Avenue. Rising 1,454 feet with 102 floors, 85 of which are occupied by offices, it has become the city's second-tallest building behind One World Trade Center, currently under construction. The Empire State's two observation decks have the highest number of visitors in the world, who come to enjoy the unparalleled 360° view of the city. Its tower lights change according to the occasion being celebrated that day, for example, patriotic blue, white, and red for July 4, and Christmas red and green for the end-of-year festivities. In late 2004, the building's lights were turned off to mark the passing of Fay Wray, the female lead in *King Kong*.

EMPIRE STATE BUILDING   Watch the trailer

350 Fifth Ave., NY 10118
Subway: 34th St.
☎ + 1 212-736-3100
http://www.esbnyc.com
Price: ★★☆☆☆

WEST VILLAGE

36	RESTAURANT	MINETTA TAVERN	*SLEEPERS*
37	RESTAURANT	CAFFE REGGIO	*INSIDE LLEWYN DAVIS*
38	RESTAURANT	JOE'S PIZZA	*SPIDER-MAN 2*
39	EXPERIENCE	TONY DAPOLITO RECREATION CENTER	*RAGING BULL*

MINETTA TAVERN
★ SLEEPERS ★

BY BARRY LEVINSON
WITH ROBERT DE NIRO, DUSTIN HOFFMAN, VITTORIO GASSMAN, KEVIN BACON, BRAD PITT
1996

The final celebration

MacDougal Street has often appeared in movies because its history is bound up with the mafia, and has been used, by extension, in stories involving criminal organizations. Not surprisingly, then, the Minetta Tavern appears in *Shaft*, *Mickey Blue Eyes*, *Godfather 2*, and *Sleepers*.

Opened in the heart of Greenwich Village in 1937, the Minetta Tavern has been frequented throughout its history by the various writers who lived in this bohemian neighborhood, such as Ernest Hemingway, Eugene O'Neill, E.E. Cummings, Dylan Thomas, and Joe Gould, as well as by mobsters during prohibition. In 2009, the establishment was taken over by Keith McNally, the famous English restaurateur based in New York, who was dubbed the "restaurateur who reinvented Downtown" following the successful launches of Schiller's and Balthazar. Preserving this institution's soul was a real challenge, but one that he has pulled off brilliantly by keeping the decor unchanged, retaining the original wood paneling and restoring the furniture. Chef William Brasile's menu delights the palates of the most demanding diners while adding new luster to the term "steakhouse."

MINETTA TAVERN

113 MacDougal St., NY 10012
Subway: W 4th St.
☎ + 1 212-475-3850
www.minettatavernny.com
Price: ★ ★ ★ ☆ ☆

Watch the trailer

CAFFE REGGIO
★ INSIDE LLEWYN DAVIS ★
BY JOEL & ETHAN COEN
WITH OSCAR ISAAC, JUSTIN TIMBERLAKE, CAREY MULLIGAN
2013

 Jean and Llewyn Davis take stock of their life together

This iconic Greenwich Village café has appeared in a number of cult movies, such as *The Godfather 2*, *Serpico*, and *Shaft*. The Coen brothers set up their cameras in this vintage establishment to convey a certain nostalgia for life in the neighborhood where Llewyn Davis is staying.

Located in the heart of Greenwich Village since 1927, Caffe Reggio is one of New York's oldest cafés—and for good reason, as it was the café's founder, Dominico Parisi, who introduced the famous Italian cappuccino to the United States. Indeed, his original espresso machine is still proudly on display inside, alongside a number of Italian paintings in memory of his native country. Of course, this national identity is also reflected in the menu, which spans breakfast and dinner and is packed with Italian classics, such as bruschetta, mozzarella, ravioli, pasta, and tiramisu, together with a few typical drinks such as amarena soda and pinot grigio. The unpretentious, cozy ambience of this address makes it a popular place with local hipsters and students. One final historical anecdote: in 1959, John Fitzgerald Kennedy delivered a campaign speech right in front of the café.

CAFFE REGGIO
119 MacDougal St., NY 10012
Subway: W 4th St.
☎ + 1 212-475-9557
www.cafereggio.com
Price: ★☆☆☆☆

Watch the trailer

The espresso machine and the Italian artworks recall the country of birth of the café's founder.

JOE'S PIZZA
★ SPIDER-MAN 2 ★

BY SAM RAIMI
WITH TOBEY MAGUIRE, KIRSTEN DUNST, JAMES FRANCO
2004

Spider-Man's first job

The aim in *Spider-Man 2* was to keep computer-generated images of the city to a minimum in order to give the superhero a human dimension, making him more ordinary than he was in the first movie. In this respect, Joe's Pizza, a Manhattan culinary institution, fit the bill perfectly. Even though the location featured in the movie closed down shortly after, the one a few doors down is just as magical.

In the space of forty years, Joe's Pizza has become a veritable Greenwich Village institution. According to *New York Magazine*, it serves the best pizza in the city, and *GC* ranked it among the top twenty-five pizzerias in the world. Its founder, Pino "Joe" Pozzuoli, who emigrated from Naples in the 1950s, has been observing pizza-eaters for fifty years with the aim of giving them what they like most. Joe makes pizzas as if he were making them for himself, so everything here is authentic. Each one is made with care, using the finest ingredients and cooked to order. Every day regulars and tourists flock to his little place for a slice of inexpensive pizza (around $3)—Plain cheese, Fresh Mozzarella, or Sicilian. The pizzeria has just a handful of tables and is frequently packed, so many eat standing up while checking out the photos on the walls of the celebrities who have stopped by for a tasty bite to eat.

JOE'S PIZZA   Watch the trailer

7 Carmine St., NY 10014-4441
Subway: Houston
☎ + 1 212-366-1182
www.joespizzanyc.com
Price: ★☆☆☆☆

THE TONY DAPOLITO RECREATION CENTER

★ RAGING BULL ★

BY MARTIN SCORSESE
WITH ROBERT DE NIRO, CATHY MORIARTY, JOE PESCI
1981

Vickie and Jake LaMotta meet

For this scene shot through wire mesh, Martin Scorsese had no trouble persuading the talented Robert De Niro, who liked to surprise his partners by changing his lines, to come up with a brilliant piece of improvisation with the inexperienced young actress Cathy Moriarty.

Initially called the Carmine Center in 1908, the sports center was renamed in 2004 as a tribute to Tony Dapolito, who worked for nearly fifty years to promote green spaces and community life in Greenwich Village. The son of Italian immigrants, he was also the owner of the wonderful bakery Vesuvio, on Prince Street, where budding sportsmen and women would go to enjoy some tasty cookies after exercising. Although you can practice a wide range of sports, including football, basketball, bocce, and even Polynesian dancing at the center, the indoor and outdoor pools, which used to be public baths (hence their shallowness), are what make the establishment so popular, particularly on sunny days. The outdoor pool will also appeal to art lovers because of the mural painted in 1990 by Keith Haring.

TONY DAPOLITO RECREATION CENTER   Watch the trailer

1 Clarkson St., NY 10014
Subway: Houston
☎ + 1 212-242-5418
www.nycgovparks.org
Price: annual subscription $75

TRIBECA

THE HARRISON
★ MICHAEL CLAYTON ★
BY TONY GILROY
WITH GEORGE CLOONEY, TOM WILKINSON, TILDA SWINTON, SYDNEY POLLACK
2007

Michael and Karen discuss the case of Arthur Edens

Director Tony Gilroy, born in New York, was determined to set his film in the urban jungle of Manhattan, amid the skyscrapers where the struggle for power and money takes place. High-end restaurant The Harrison, frequented by affluent diners, fit the bill perfectly.

Following the success of his Chelsea restaurant The Red Cat, Jimmy Bradley opened The Harrison in 2001 in the heart of Tribeca, where it quickly became an institution for the neighborhood's movers and shakers. First off, it is a welcoming place, with the kind of impeccable, highly attentive service prized by the people who come here. The cozy atmosphere is enhanced by soft lighting, while the elegant decor combining wood paneling and white walls is very Tribeca. Diners lap up the inventive, sophisticated cuisine, with its Mediterranean and American accents, which can be paired with local wines carefully selected to ensure a perfect match. Finally, in spring and summer, The Harrison's outdoor tables are another big draw.

THE HARRISON   Watch the trailer

355 Greenwich St., NY 10013
Subway: Franklin St.
☎ + 1 212-274-9310
www.theharrison.com
Price: ★★★☆☆

BUBBY'S

★ THE DEVIL WEARS PRADA ★

BY DAVID FRANKEL
WITH MERYL STREEP, ANNE HATHAWAY, EMILY BLUNT, STANLEY TUCCI
2006

Andy and her friends get together in a restaurant

With its red-brick facade, its wide windows where the table that was to appear in the film could be positioned, and its location at a busy intersection frequented by yellow taxi cabs, Bubby's illustrated perfectly the hustle and bustle of New York that the director was looking for.

Bubby's started life in 1990 as a wholesale pie company, but following its success it quickly morphed into a restaurant. Its old chairs, unique coffee percolator, and wood-fired oven indispensable for the cooking of its pies have made it Tribeca's favorite address. Although the place has grown since the early days, and its popularity extends beyond the confines of Manhattan, Bubby's has stayed true to its original values, with a menu that features simple, traditional, homemade American fare served in a flea market decor. Every dish is based on a traditional recipe and uses the finest ingredients. Not surprisingly, the tarts and cakes are as irresistible as ever, and the salad with anchovy dressing makes a perfect lunch, but the highlight is the weekend brunch: a Bubby's Breakfast followed by a Flaky Biscuit won't be soon forgotten.

BUBBY'S

120 Hudson St., NY 10013
Subway: Franklin St.
☎ + 1 212-219-0666
www.bubbys.com
Price: ★★☆☆☆

Watch the trailer

HOOK & LADDER 8
★ GHOSTBUSTERS ★
BY VAN REITMAN
WITH BILL MURRAY, DAN AYKROYD, HAROLD RAMIS, SIGOURNEY WEAVER, RICK MORANIS
1984

The Ghostbusters' headquarters

This firehouse in Tribeca, with its distinctive red brickwork, was designed in 1895 by the fire department's superintendent of buildings, Alexander H. Stevens, who was in charge of designing the city's firehouses. But it is above all the Ghostbusters logo painted on the sidewalk that gets the cameras snapping every day. Ironically, even though Hook & Ladder 8 was one of the first firehouses to dispatch its men to try to save lives at the World Trade Center, thanks to the power of cinema it is still known around the world for its role in *Ghostbusters*. Being in the limelight isn't all roses, however. In 2011, Mayor Michael Bloomberg decided to close the firehouse as a result of budget cuts. Protests by New Yorkers led to a change of heart, but for how long?...

Because it was in use when the film was shot, the famous building, with its typical New York facade, only appeared in the outdoor scenes. The indoor scenes were shot in a fire station in the heart of Downtown Los Angeles that had been disused since the 1960s.

HOOK & LADDER 8   Watch the trailer
14 N. Moore St., NY 10013
Subway : Franklin St.
Price: ☆☆☆☆☆

WALKER'S
★ NEW YORK, I LOVE YOU ★
BY JIANG WEN
WITH RACHEL BILSON, HAYDEN CHRISTENSEN, ANDY GARCIA
2010

When the theft of a wallet turns into romantic rivalry

Walker's restaurant, which opened in Tribeca in 1880, has survived for one and a half centuries, all the while retaining the look of a classic bar from another age. Its long, slightly worn counter, the old black and white photos of New York on the walls, and the patina on its high pressed-tin ceiling add a touch of nostalgia to this welcoming place. Neighborhood office workers converge here after work to enjoy one of the ten draft beers served, mingling with locals come to enjoy traditional dishes such as *steak au poivre* with potatoes or grilled vegetables, or the roast salmon with herbs, asparagus, chickpeas, and cherry tomatoes. A large selection of wines is available to accompany the food, which is served by friendly staff. Walker's is also open at lunchtime for a tasty sandwich or a burger.

Walker's serves as a backdrop to the first section of the film, fulfilling one of the creative conditions imposed on the eleven directors, namely that each story had to make it possible to identify visually one or several New York neighborhoods. Mission accomplished for Jiang Wen thanks to the choice of this delightfully atmospheric Tribeca eatery.

WALKER'S   Watch the trailer

16 N. Moore St., NY 10013
Subway: Franklin St.
☎ + 1 212-941-0142
www.walkersnyc.com
Price: ★★☆☆☆

SNACK
★ LAST NIGHT ★
BY MASSY TADJEDIN
WITH KEIRA KNIGHTLEY, EVA MENDES, SAM WORTHINGTON, GUILLAUME CANET
2011

Joanna comes across Alex as she goes to get coffee

In the same way that she chose a cosmopolitan cast (Eva Mendes is Cuban, Guillaume Canet French, Keira Knightley English, and Sam Worthington Australian), Iranian-American director Massy Tadjedin picked New York for its diversity, filming only in places that had an international resonance.

This place has a very misleading name for what is in fact a full-fledged restaurant in the heart of Soho. On the other side of the facade's little window, you can taste authentic samples of the best of traditional Hellenic cuisine. The home-made *tzatziki*, *meze*, *skordalia*, and pies (notably the chicken, feta, and onion) are a delight for the taste buds. The narrow interior with its minimalist rustic decor has five simple wooden tables and white walls adorned with timeless photos. The regulars who live in the neighborhood also come here for Greek coffee. We particularly recommend the Sunday brunch, with its scrambled eggs served with grilled tomatoes in pita bread. In addition, you can buy a selection of Greek products, such as delicious wines, sherry, honey, and other delicacies—a sure cure for homesickness.

SNACK   Watch the trailer

105 Thompson St., NY 10012
Subway: Prince St.
☎ + 1 212-925-1040
http://www.snacksoho.com
Price: ★★☆☆☆

DEAN & DELUCA
★ JULIE & JULIA ★

BY NORA EPHRON
WITH MERYL STREEP, AMY ADAMS, STANLEY TUCCI, CHRIS MESSINA, EMMANUEL SUAREZ
2009

 *Julie stocks up on cheese*

It was impossible to exclude Dean & DeLuca, that most iconic of gourmet stores, from this film dealing with the culinary arts. It was here, of course, that Julie, a budding chef, had to shop for food.

In 1977, Giorgio DeLuca, a cheese merchant, and Joel Dean, a publisher, opened their first Dean & DeLuca store in Soho. Their dream was to create a temple to the finest foods in New York. Combining new culinary trends such as balsamic vinegar and dried tomatoes—which they were the first to import—with traditional dishes ready to cook or already cooked (to perfection), such as the sublime meatloaf with roast carrots and fennel, this excellence quickly found favor. In 1986 the store moved to its current premises, covering 10,000 square feet, where a cornucopia of food and cooking utensils is magnificently arranged in a minimalist Neoclassical decor, with exposed columns, Carrara marble floor, steel shelves, white-tiled walls, and impeccable display cases that make you want to sample everything, or at the very least pick up a snack at the take-out counter before continuing with your shopping. Take advantage of the extended open hours; the store gets very crowded at lunchtime.

DEAN & DELUCA   Watch the trailer

560 Broadway, NY 10012
Subway: Prince St.
☎ + 1 212-226-6800
www.deandeluca.com
Price: ★★☆☆☆

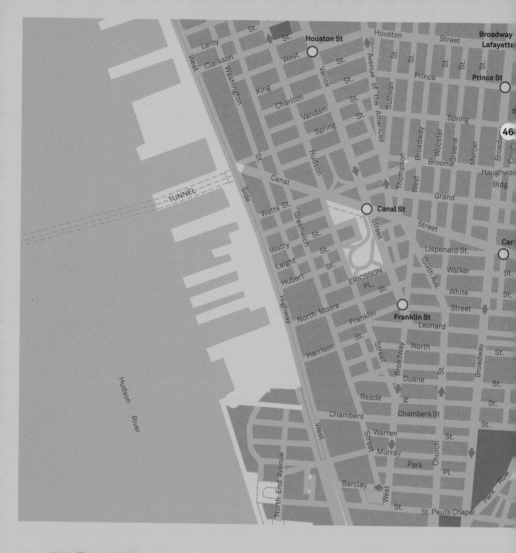

NOLITA – LOWER EAST SIDE

BALTHAZAR
★ HOLLYWOOD ENDING ★

BY WOODY ALLEN
WITH WOODY ALLEN, DEBRA MESSING, TÉA LEONI, TREAT WILLIAMS, TIFFANI THIESSEN
2002

An unexpected reunion in a restaurant

Opened in 1997 by Keith McNally, this restaurant, with its Belle Époque decor of red leather banquettes and wide mirrors, resembles a Parisian brasserie. The French touch also extends to the menu, where you'll find snails, onion soup, *confit de canard*, and *moules frites*. But the standout dish is the *steak frites*, which is served around 200 times a day. The desserts also have a Gallic inflection, with *tarte tatin* and chocolate profiteroles. Not surprisingly, the wines and champagnes are worthy of a fine French restaurant. Balthazar has its own bakery, too, which is very popular at breakfast time, for its bread as well as its pastries. Frequented by locals and tourists alike, Balthazar is also a sought-after celebrity spot, so you are strongly advised to book ahead or risk facing a two-hour wait. Its success here in Soho led to the creation of an outpost in London where a new Balthazar opened in early 2013.

Woody Allen, a regular here, immortalized the ambience at Balthazar, which can also be seen in the credits of *Hitch*, starring Will Smith and Eva Mendes.

BALTHAZAR   Watch the trailer

80 Spring St., NY 10012
Subway: Spring St.
☎ + 1 212-965-1414
www.balthazarny.com
Price: ★ ★ ★ ☆ ☆

RICE TO RICHES
★ HITCH ★
BY ANDY TENNANT
WITH WILL SMITH, EVA MENDES, KEVIN JAMES
2005

📹 *Sara talks about her first date with Hitch*

For this movie set in New York, director Andy Tennant wanted to focus on the unknown heart of Manhattan, and in particular the Tribeca and Soho neighborhoods. He deliberately featured some distinctive addresses that are off the beaten track, such as Rice to Riches, where nobody had ever filmed before.

What on earth inspired Peter Moceo, the founder of Rice to Riches, to open a rice pudding fast-food place? Was there really a demand for it? We loved the facade as soon as we saw it: with its pop colors, it really stands out in this neighborhood dominated by vintage storefronts. This amusing store, with its futuristic interior, is all about having fun. The walls are enlivened by quotations such as *Fat... happens* and *Big is beautiful*, which are clearly intended to put calorie junkies at ease. But perhaps the cleverest thing about the venture was getting Jemal Edwards, former head pastry chef at Nobu and Montrachet, to come up with a host of recipes bearing such improbable names and flavors as "Coconut Coma" and "Sex, Drugs, and Rocky Road," which can be coated in almonds or chocolate chips, depending on your mood. At this one-of-a-kind shop, you'll feel like a kid again.

RICE TO RICHES   Watch the trailer

37 Spring St., NY 10012
Subway: Spring St.
☎ + 1 212-274-0008
www.ricetoriches.com
Price: ★☆☆☆☆

This quirky store has a playful, futurist decor.

LITTLE CUPCAKE BAKESHOP
★ NOUS YORK ★

BY GÉRALDINE NAKACHE & HERVÉ MIMRAN
WITH LEÏLA BEKHTI, GÉRALDINE NAKACHE, MANU PAYET, SIENNA MILLER
2012

Gabrielle and Samia cannot resist buying cupcakes

Every woman visiting New York has to have one of these cupcakes. It was only natural, then, that Géraldine Nakache and Leila Bekhti be filmed at this store's checkout, facing Maria Dizzia playing a rather over-zealous shop assistant.

The first Little Cupcake Bakeshop opened in Brooklyn on July 23, 2005, by four brothers from the neighborhood. Their philosophy was to offer traditional American desserts made from fresh seasonal produce supplied by small regional producers, in a green, environment-friendly store. The concept was a big hit, and a second store appeared in the trendy Nolita neighborhood. As the name suggests, this bakery sells cupcakes, those little cakes that were very popular in the 1950s and that had fallen out of fashion until they were resurrected by the series *Sex and the City*. They come in a variety of flavors, from Blue Velvet with blueberries, to Peanut Butter & Jelly. There are even sugar-free versions for calorie-conscious fashionistas. If you're feeling rebellious, there are other kinds of goodies to choose from, such as cheesecake and pies, like Pecan Pie, Key Lime (in the summer), and Pumpkin Pie (in the fall), as well as all kinds of other cakes, including Carrot Cake.

LITTLE CUPCAKE BAKESHOP

30 Prince St., NY 10012
Subway: Prince St.
☎ + 1 212-941-9100
www.littlecupcakebakeshop.com
Price: ★★☆☆☆

Watch the trailer

Cupcakes in a multitude of flavors.

CAFÉ HABANA
★ FRIENDS WITH BENEFITS ★
BY WILL GLUCK
WITH JUSTIN TIMBERLAKE, MILA KUNIS
2011

A lunch break for Justin and Mila

Passionate about romantic comedies from the golden age of Hollywood, the director was determined to feature solely iconic New York places in his movie. That is how the Café Habana, adored by connoisseurs, including regular Justin Timberlake, ended up being invited to audition.

The Café Habana was created in 1998 by Sean Meenan, who was inspired by a luncheonette in Mexico said to have been the haunt of Che Guevara and Fidel Castro, who plotted the Cuban revolution there. Fifteen years later, this tiny, unpretentious restaurant has become a hangout for hipsters, celebrities, and other fans of Cuban cuisine, who are happy to join the line of people from breakfast to dinner waiting for one of the sought-after tables. The tasty cooking, generous servings, and reasonable prices ensure that this place is permanently full. The fish tacos, Cuban pork sandwich—voted the best in New York—and tender chicken quesadilla will make you an instant fan. On the drinks front, the mojito and margarita both come in explosive versions. The impeccable service and laid-back atmosphere make for a supremely relaxing experience that you will not want to end.

CAFÉ HABANA   Watch the trailer

17 Prince St., NY 10012
Subway: Spring St.
☎ + 1 212-625-2001
www.cafehabana.com
Price: ★☆☆☆☆

YONAH SCHIMMEL KNISH BAKERY
★ WHATEVER WORKS ★

BY WOODY ALLEN
WITH LARRY DAVID, EVAN RACHEL WOOD
2009

Melody wonders about the content of a knish

A trip to New York is always a good opportunity to eat local food. Having sampled a pastrami sandwich, a Black and White Cookie, and some cheesecake, why not try a knish? For your first experience of this turnover made of puff pastry filled with potato, one place stands out: the Yonah Schimmel Knish Bakery, whose motto is "One World, One Taste, One Knish. That's It." When he arrived from Eastern Europe in 1890, Yonah opened a store with his cousin Joseph Berger in the Lower East Side, which was a Jewish neighborhood at the time. In 1910, the store moved to its present address. Six generations later, the place has stayed the same while the neighborhood has become a trendy enclave of New York nightlife. This has been a boon for the knishery: its usual clientele has expanded with young people and tourists, who come to hang out in the back room from morning to evening as they fill their tummies with tasty knishes and the other house specialties, such as potato pancakes and blintzes.

Woody Allen, one of the Yonah Schimmel Knish Bakery's regulars, featured the store in his film, poking fun at the legend according to which no one really knows what's in a knish.

YONAH SCHIMMEL KNISH BAKERY   Watch the trailer

137 E. Houston St., NY 10002
Subway: 2nd Ave.
☎ + 1 212-477-2858
www.knishery.com
Price: ★☆☆☆☆

KATZ'S DELICATESSEN
★ WHEN HARRY MET SALLY ★
BY ROB REINER
WITH BILLY CRYSTAL, MEG RYAN
1989

🎥 *Sally's loud, personal demonstration*

Katz's, founded in 1888, is one of the oldest, most legendary delis in Manhattan. It became popular in the early 20th century, when hundreds of thousands of Jewish immigrant families fresh from Europe lived on the Lower East Side. Katz's quickly became the ideal local restaurant for people to meet up in. During World War II, the owner's three sons left to fight for their country, giving rise to the motto that has been displayed in the establishment ever since: "Send a salami to your boy in the Army." The menu upholds tradition by serving kosher cuisine, with dishes ordered at the counter. The pastrami sandwich on rye made by this veritable institution is reputed to be the best in New York.

The film is remembered above all for the expressive orgasm that Sally fakes before an astounded Harry. Screenwriter Nora Ephron created this hilarious scene because she was concerned that the movie had been weighted too much in favor of the male character's role since the beginning of the story. Not to be outdone, Rob Reiner then came up with the famous line from the neighboring table, "I'll have what she's having!" It was uttered by his own mother, who was an extra.

KATZ'S DELICATESSEN   Watch the trailer

205 E. Houston St., NY 10002
Subway: 2nd Ave.
☎ + 1 212-254-2246
www.katzsdelicatessen.com
Price: ★★☆☆☆

AZUL
★ FRANCES HA ★
BY NOAH BAUMBACH
WITH GRETA GERWIG, MICKEY SUMNER, MICHAEL ESPER, ADAM DRIVER
2013

🎥 *Trouble paying the bill*

The restaurant Azul, located in the heart of the Lower East Side, lent its endearing personality and bohemian ambience to this movie, in which the heroine, like thousands of other artists and performers in New York, faces a daily struggle for a place in the sun.

Opened in 2001, Azul's Argentine roots and warm atmosphere contributed to the revitalization of the Lower East Side at a time when the city was going through one of the darkest periods in its history. This vibrant, attractive place has bare brick walls adorned with advertising signs that add local color, including one advertising Quilmes Argentine beer. With its chic bistro vibe, it has plenty of attractive features that keep its customers coming back. The ceiling is plastered with newspaper pages, while a shrine pays tribute to soccer demigod Maradona. Candles flicker cozily on the tables as you wait for your main course: particularly tender, roasted, braised, or grilled meat, cooked to taste. Best of all are the *empanadas*: served as appetizers, these house specialties are made with puff pastry filled with beef, chicken, spinach, or cheese, and draw many New Yorkers all the way across town.

AZUL ARGENTINE BISTRO   Watch the trailer

152 Stanton St., NY 10002
Subway: Houston
☎ + 1 646-602-2004
www.azulnyc.com
Price: ★★★☆☆

SCHILLER'S LIQUOR BAR
★ MORNING GLORY ★

BY ROGER MICHELL
WITH RACHEL MCADAMS, HARRISON FORD, DIANE KEATON, JEFF GOLDBLUM, PATRICK WILSON
2011

Becky flees from her breakfast with Adam

Roger Michell's film could only have been shot in New York, which is famous for its morning TV shows, as well as being the city that symbolizes American ambition, embodied by the character of Becky. To provide a contrast with the stressful environment of the *Daybreak* TV studio, the director filmed his young producers at the cool Schiller's Liquor Bar, where the atmosphere is less intense.

Schiller's Liquor Bar was opened in 2003 by Keith McNally, who transformed abandoned premises in the Lower East Side into a hot new restaurant with a laid-back vibe. With its yellow neon lights, white-tiled walls, and Tolix© chairs, this quintessential New York eatery has all the ingredients to be a magnet for trend-setters. You can sit at the bar and sip a cocktail or grab a table and choose from a menu of solid, inexpensive American fare, ranging from the Schiller's *steak frites* or macaroni and cheese with bacon to the cheeseburger. Schiller's also offers a selection of European wines, divided into three clever categories: *Cheap*, *Decent*, and *Good*. Finally, the address is open from early in the morning to late at night, much to the delight of night owls.

SCHILLER'S LIQUOR BAR   Watch the trailer

131 Rivington St., NY 10002
Subway: Bowery
☎ + 1 212-260-4555
www.schillersny.com
Price: ★★☆☆☆

IRVING FARM COFFEE ROASTERS
★ CHINESE PUZZLE ★

BY CÉDRIC KLAPISCH
WITH ROMAIN DURIS, CÉCILE DE FRANCE, AUDREY TAUTOU, KELLY REILLY
2013

🎥 *Isabelle tells Xavier that she is attracted to the babysitter*

Cédric Klapisch chose the Lower East Side for his movie, creating an authentic portrait of this part of New York where he lived when he was studying filmmaking. Thanks to such typical places as 88 Orchard Street, he succeeded in capturing the neighborhood's ambience.

Originally opened in a tiny space near Union Square in 1996, Irving Farm's mission is to offer good-quality coffee from beans they roast themselves in old farm buildings they acquired in 1999 in the Hudson Valley. The business's original concept, which puts the emphasis on dealing directly with producers, quickly proved a hit in Manhattan, where they now have four stores, notably this pretty one in Orchard Street, where the red-brick walls, industrial-style wooden furniture, and large windows are a constant reminder that you are in New York. Of course, regulars come for their precious morning energy boost in the form of an espresso or Americano and a muffin, but the place also offers lunchtime eats in the form of organic salads and sandwiches, such as the delicious roast chicken and avocado, made on multi-grain bread. You can also leave with a bag of the famous house coffee, which is available for sale.

IRVING FARM COFFEE ROASTERS

88 Orchard St., NY 10002
Subway: Delancey St.
☎+1 212-228-8880
www.irvingfarm.com
Price: ★★☆☆☆

Watch the trailer

Hudson River

Duane St

Broad St

Broad St

Reade St

W. St

Chambers Chambers St

St.

Warren St.

Street

West

Murray St.

North End Avenue

Park Pl.

Church St

Barclay St

West St.

Park Row

St. Paul's Chapel

North Cove

WTC Fulton St.

New World Trade Center

Cortlandt St

Maiden

North Cove

Liberty St

Battery Cedar St

ONE LIBERTY PLAZA

Nassau St.

Trinity

Albany St

Pine St.

Waterfront Promenade

Highway

Wall St

William

Park

RECTOR PLACE

St. Broad St

City

Rector Rector St

Wall St

W. Thames St.

Broadway

Broad

South Cove

THIRD PL.

BOWLING GREEN

56

SECOND PL.

Beaver St.

Whitehall

Bowling Green

BATTERY PL.

State St.

Pearl St.

W. Se

Battery Park

BROOKLYN BATTERY TUNNEL

P. MINUIT PLAZA

M

South Ferry

58

57

LOWER MANHATTAN

BROOKLYN BRIDGE
★ I AM LEGEND ★
BY FRANCIS LAWRENCE
WITH WILL SMITH
2007

 The attack on Manhattan

A symbol of America, the Brooklyn Bridge has often been put through the mill in such disaster movies as *Godzilla*, *Armageddon*, *Deep Impact*, *Independence Day*, *The Day After Tomorrow*, and *Cloverfield*. The scene filmed for *I Am Legend*, which involved 1,000 extras and six nights of filming, holds the record for being the most expensive scene ever shot in New York, costing five million dollars.

Along with the Empire State Building and the Statue of Liberty, the Brooklyn Bridge is one of New York's most iconic structures. Its legendary appearance was the work of engineer John Augustus Roebling, who died shortly after construction had started. This tragedy heralded fourteen years of setbacks until the completion of its ground-breaking design, which was subsequently copied throughout the country. For example, the two towers rising above the East River had to be laid 40-80 feet beneath the surface of the water, which resulted in around 27 deaths due to decompression. This architectural saga was brought to a close with its inauguration in 1883. Today, the structure's solidity is not in doubt: every day, more than 150,000 vehicles and pedestrians cross the bridge that links Manhattan to Brooklyn and offers an unrivaled view.

BROOKLYN BRIDGE   Watch the trailer
Subway: Brooklyn Br./Chambers St.
www.nyc.gov
Price: ☆☆☆☆☆

DELMONICO'S
★ THE APRIL FOOLS ★
BY STUART ROSENBERG
WITH CATHERINE DENEUVE, JACK LEMMON, PETER LAWFORD, JACK WESTON
1969

 *Confiding in a friend*

A veritable New York gastronomic institution, Delmonico's offers the kind of lavish dining experience you would expect of a Financial District restaurant frequented by Wall Street bankers. It was a natural location for director Stuart Rosenberg to film the young, newly promoted businessman Jack Lemmon confiding in a friend and colleague about his romantic escapades.

When they opened for business in 1827 in the heart of the future Wall Street district, the Delmonico brothers could hardly have anticipated that their small coffee, wine, and Havana cigar store would become one of New York's leading culinary destinations. The success of their business led them to expand operations in 1837, opening Manhattan's first gastronomic restaurant, where chef Fellipini created the specialty with which it has become synonymous: the Delmonico steak. Thanks to the genius of the French chef Charles Ranhofer, the restaurant would go on to invent dishes that would become classics around the world, such as Eggs Benedict, Chicken a la Keene (which later evolved into Chicken a la King) and Baked Alaska. All of these delights are still on the menu of this restaurant, which has not lost one iota of its prestige.

DELMONICO'S   Watch the trailer

56 Beaver St., NY 10004
Subway: Wall St.
☎+1 212-509-1144
www.delmonicosny.com
Price: ★★★★★

THE STATUE OF LIBERTY
★ TITANIC ★
BY JAMES CAMERON
WITH KATE WINSLET, LEONARDO DICAPRIO
1998

🎥◄ *The Carpathia arrives in New York Bay*

The Statue of Liberty was always the first thing that immigrants arriving in New York by ship would see, and the movie remains true to history, with the monument appearing as an ineluctable symbol at the end.

Liberty Enlightening the World, known worldwide as the "Statue of Liberty," was made in France and presented as a gift to America in 1876 to celebrate the centennial of its independence. Inspired by the Colossus of Rhodes, this masterpiece was created by the sculptor Frédéric Bartholdi, assisted by Gustave Eiffel for the structure. It rests on a base designed by Richard Morris Hunt, which raises the gilded torch almost 305 feet in the air. The statue stands on Liberty Island, not far from Ellis Island, where immigrants arriving in America in the late 19th century were processed (and which is now home to a museum devoted to their experience). She faces Paris, where, on the other side of the Atlantic, a miniature replica near the Pont de Grenelle in turn faces her. The inside of the statue is open to visitors. Although tickets can be booked in advance, you may still have to wait in line before entering the bowels of the myth.

STATUE OF LIBERTY   Watch the trailer

Liberty Island, NY 10004
Subway: South Ferry
☎ + 1 212-363-3200
www.nps.gov
Price: ★☆☆☆☆

ELLIS ISLAND
★ THE IMMIGRANT ★

BY JAMES GRAY
WITH MARION COTILLARD, JOAQUIN PHOENIX, JEREMY RENNER
2013

 *Ewa and Magda arrive in America*

James Gray wanted to recreate exactly what it was like for immigrants arriving at Ellis Island in 1921. To this end, he had to assemble on the island more than one thousand extras and a two-hundred-strong crew for two nights of intense filming.

Initially a military site, it was in 1892 that the little island was turned into a federal immigration station where new arrivals in America were processed. They had previously been received at a center in what is now Battery Park, which had become unable to cope with the growing numbers. As the film reveals, new arrivals had to be in perfect health when they arrived at Ellis Island, or else risk being sent straight back or having to spend several months in quarantine on the island. Every immigrant had already answered a detailed questionnaire that was carefully examined before they could even set sail for America, the land of hope. Between January 1, 1892, when it opened, and its closure on November 12, 1954, the center processed more than 12 million candidates. The island is today listed on the National Register of Historic Places and is home to a museum tracing the history of immigration with photos, objects and touching personal stories from the period.

ELLIS ISLAND

Ellis Island, NY 10004
Subway: South Ferry
☎ + 1 212-363-3200
www.ellisisland.org
Price: ★☆☆☆☆

Watch the trailer

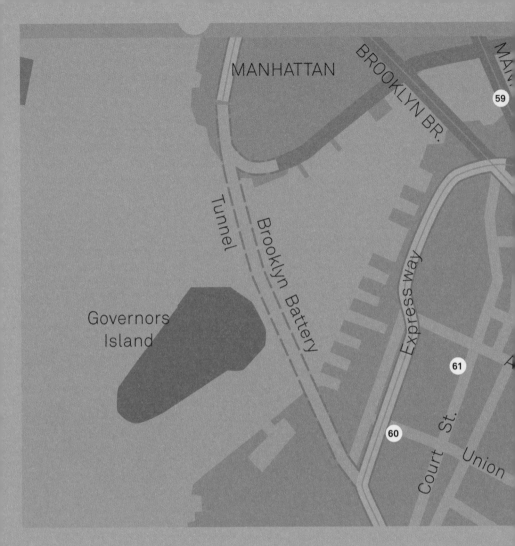

MANHATTAN

BROOKLYN BR.

MAN

59

Tunnel

Brooklyn Battery

Governors
Island

Express way

61

A

Court St.

60

Union

BROOKLYN

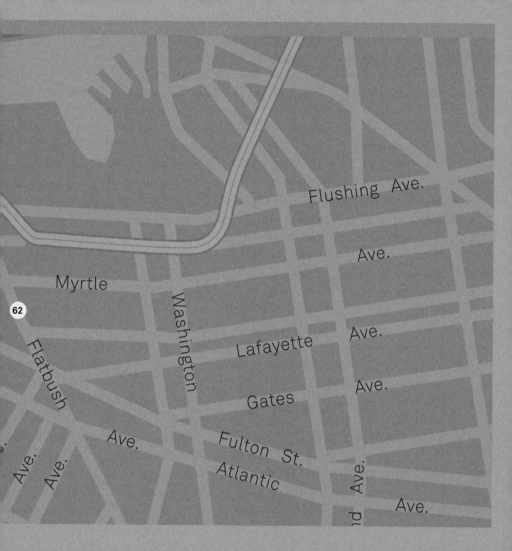

MANHATTAN BRIDGE
★ ONCE UPON A TIME IN AMERICA ★
BY SERGIO LEONE
WITH ROBERT DE NIRO, JAMES WOODS
1984

 Childhood memories

The bridge, which links the Dumbo ("Down under the Manhattan Bridge overpass") neighborhood with Manhattan, added a symbolic dimension to the film by yoking together two different social worlds. The image used in the poster, which is from the final scene of the movie, immortalizes the intersection of Water Street and Washington Street in Brooklyn.

The bridge was built with the aim of improving traffic flow into Manhattan by relieving pressure on its predecessors, the Brooklyn and Williamsburg bridges. Construction took more than five years and was marked by dark dealings and rejected engineering proposals before Leon Moisseiff completed it in 1909. Until 1940, it was used by cars, subway trains, and streetcars. After numerous extensive repairs were carried out to make the bridge safer, its two decks are now used by cars, buses, and trucks on the upper level, while subway tracks, a bike lane, and pedestrian walkway share the lower level. A remarkable archway on the Manhattan side, inspired by the Porte Saint-Denis in Paris, adds a certain grandeur as you head onto the bridge; the other one, on the Brooklyn side, was removed to improve traffic flow. A word of warning to acrophobes: the pedestrian walkway tends to sway, even when there is no wind.

MANHATTAN BRIDGE   Watch the trailer
Subway: York St.
www.nyc.gov
Price: ☆☆☆☆☆

FERDINANDO'S FOCACCERIA

★ THE DEPARTED ★

BY MARTIN SCORSESE
WITH LEONARDO DICAPRIO, MATT DAMON, JACK NICHOLSON, VERA FARMIGA, MARK WAHLBERG
2006

Billy questions Madeleine about Colin

Although the story takes place in Boston, only the outdoor scenes were actually shot there. Martin Scorsese used Brooklyn, which is architecturally similar, for the indoor scenes.

Ferdinando's Focacceria opened in 1904 in a part of Brooklyn that was the stronghold of Sicilian dockers, providing them with inexpensive Italian cuisine. While the neighborhood's population may have changed since then, the restaurant has remained the same. As soon as you enter, you are struck by the hundred-year-old press clippings on the walls and the floor's mosaic tiles that make you feel like you've traveled through time. But Ferdinando's legendary status is based above all on its authentic dishes. Although everything is excellent, we recommend the following specialties: the *arancini*, rice balls stuffed with meat and chickpeas; the special *panelle*, chickpea fritters topped with ricotta and sprinkled with Parmesan; and finally the astonishing *vastedda*, a roll filled with braised veal spleen and topped with ricotta and pecorino, a symbol of Palermo's working-class culinary habits. Just like in the old days, the portions are generous and the prices modest.

FERDINANDO'S FOCACCERIA   Watch the trailer

151 Union Street, Brooklyn, NY 11231
Subway: Carroll St.
☎+1 718-855-1545
www.ferdinandosfocacceria.com
Price: ★☆☆☆☆

BOOKCOURT
★ EAT PRAY LOVE ★

BY RYAN MURPHY
WITH JULIA ROBERTS, RICHARD JENKINS, JAVIER BARDEM, JAMES FRANCO
2010

Julia Roberts buys an Italian phrase book

When Henry Zook and Mary Gannett opened BookCourt in the fall of 1981, it was just a small independent bookstore run by enthusiasts. Thirty years and a few additional square feet later, it remains a family business that continues to offer a wide selection of books. It has strengthened its roots in the neighborhood by regularly inviting local writers to meet their readers, and its 30% discount on bestsellers is as popular as ever. Voted New York's best independent bookstore in 2012 by both *The Village Voice* and *Time Out*, BookCourt has been one of the Big Apple's preeminent independent bookstores and continues to set the pace: there is currently talk of a bar at the rear of the store where wine and beer will be served, together with locally produced goodies.

For the director, Brooklyn had the perfect ambience for the film's bookstore scene (his heroine lived in a New York suburb), and BookCourt, because it is so woven into the neighborhood's DNA, was the obvious choice. The store is usually open 365 days a year, but on that particular day it made an exception so that the scene could be filmed.

BOOKCOURT   Watch the trailer

163 Court St., Brooklyn, NY 11201
Subway: Carroll St.
☎ + 1 718-875-3677
bookcourt.com
Price: ★☆☆☆☆

JUNIOR'S
★ SEX AND THE CITY ★
BY MICHAEL PATRICK KING
WITH SARAH JESSICA PARKER, KIM CATTRALL, CYNTHIA NIXON, KRISTIN DAVIS, CHRIS NOTH
2008

Carrie and Mr. Big celebrate with friends after their wedding

If this movie had a moral, it would resemble one from a fairy tale: your name might be Carrie Bradshaw and you might just have married Mr. Big, but you can still be down-to-earth. This is what the film's happy end teaches us by having the newlyweds' wedding meal take place at Junior's, a monument to working-class cuisine in New York.

Junior's is far more than just a restaurant; it's an institution whose address is passed around confidentially, like some family secret. To begin with, this place, whose facade is unchanged since the 1950s and extends for nearly a quarter of a block, is a family restaurant. So long diner, welcome to the real America! Timeless signs in the windows display the best cheesecake in the state. Available for takeout (highly recommended!), it's incredibly popular and should not be missed. But equally worth exploring is the dining area, with its multicolored benches and a menu catering to every taste, with prices that remain low. From the Southern fried chicken breast, served with mashed potato, gravy, and corn on the cob, to the turkey, corned beef, and pastrami sandwich, the food here is a treat for the taste buds. To top things off, the service is impeccable. You will leave sated—and sad that the meal is over.

JUNIOR'S   Watch the trailer

386 Flatbush Ave. Extension, Brooklyn,
NY 11201
Subway: Dekalb Ave.
☎ + 1 718-852-5257
www.juniorscheesecake.com
Price: ★☆☆☆☆

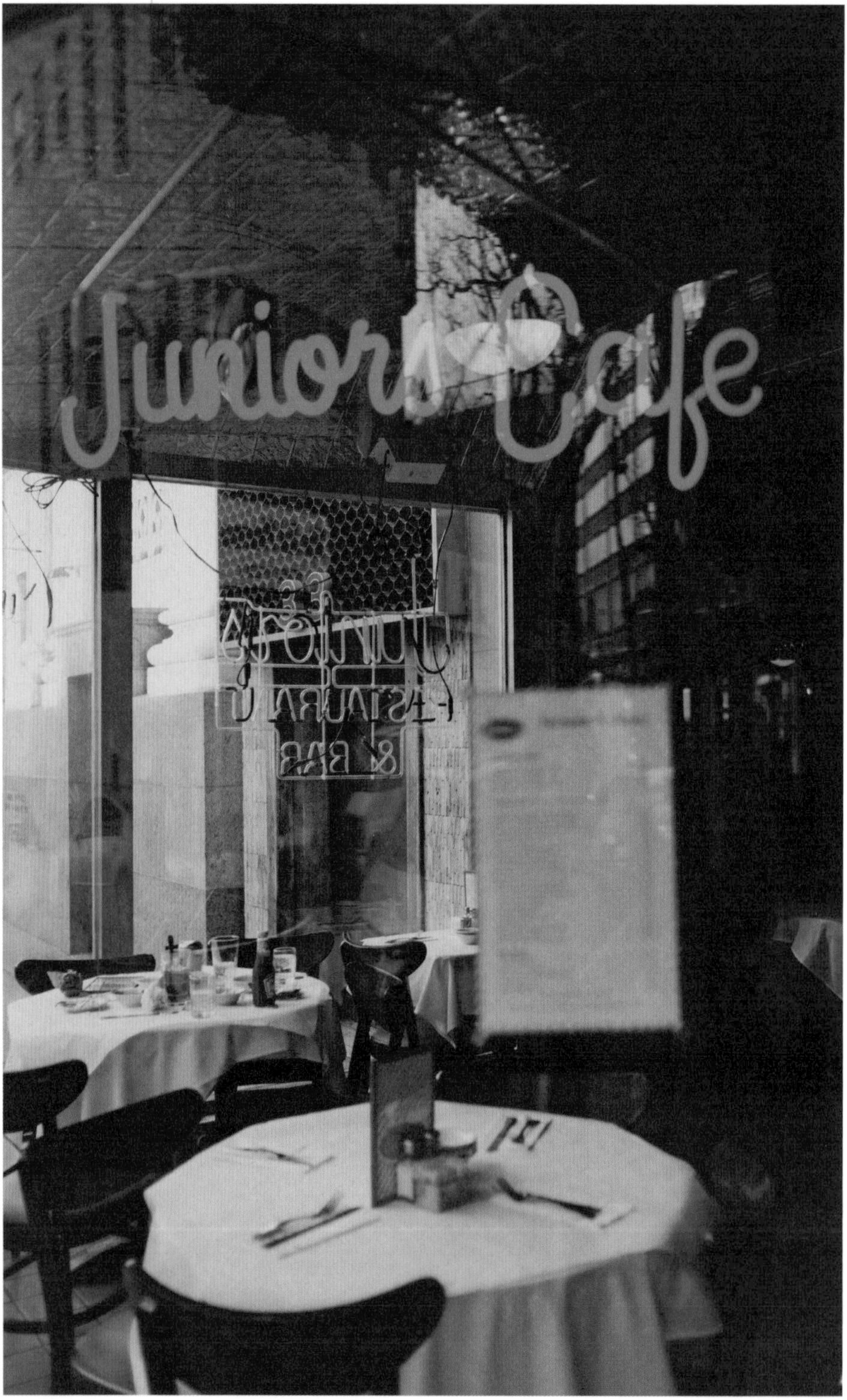
Junior's Cafe
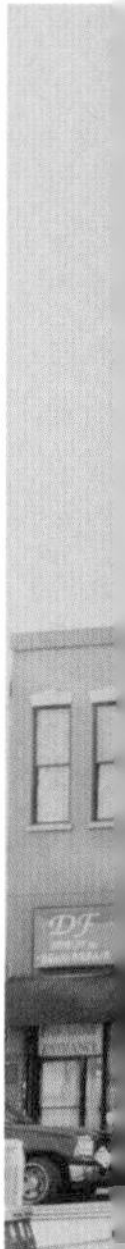
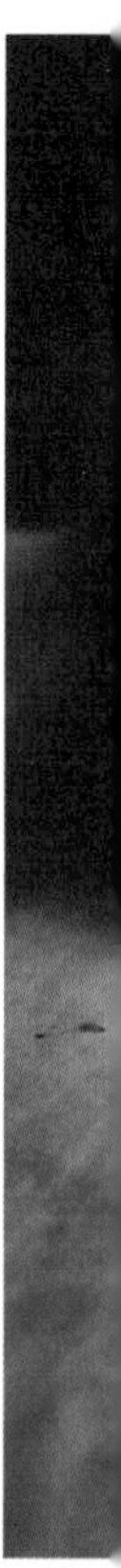

A menu that caters to all appetites, at always affordable prices.

INDEX

INDEX

ACKNOWLEDGEMENTS

Eternal devotion to our fairy godmother Virginie, who swept aside our doubts and enabled our dreams to take flight.

Unswerving friendship to David: as you can see, we actually produced this guide to New York!

Deepest gratitude to Sévérine and Bruno, who opened up the gates of the fortified kingdom of publishing to us.

A heartfelt thought for Pierre-Olivier: we really missed you in New York, even though you made the trip with us in our hearts.

Infinite thanks to Isabelle (alias Princess Zaza) and Steve, whose luminous photos saved some of the places in this guide.

Gratitude to Fabienne, Flavie, and Sabine for their support and guidance in bringing our series to fruition.

Deepest respect for Constance, Florence, Pierre C., Jean-Philippe, Philippe, and Pierre L., who never confused this dream with our real life.

A special thought for Amélie, Yannick, Antoine, Rémi, and Edouard, and their enthusiastic encouragement as we pursued this venture.

All-encompassing love to our Stars and their tender patience as they watched us run, even further than before.

Boundless affection for our dear parents and their constant and serene confidence in supporting our projects, even the craziest ones.

FAIT SON

Cinéma

LA FABRIQUE D'EXPERIENCES DU 7°ART

Did you enjoy it? Do you want more?
Join us in uncovering new places
in Paris and around the world on :
www.parisfaitsoncinema.com

1 new challenge, 2 irrepressible smiles, 4 sleeves rolled up,
2 dog-eared Harrap's©, 1 memorable Festival du Film Américain de Deauville,
2 unlimited movie passes, 2 blu-ray players, 468 films analyzed,
237 put on the shortlist, 1,924 hours to find the addresses,
2 international phone cards, 6 Paris–New York return tickets, 5 pairs of sneakers,
0 luggage lost or on-board incidents, 4 Metrocards©, 2 street maps,
1 case of acrophobia bravely overcome, 1 blizzard, 1 hundred kilometers on foot,
3 new squirrel friends, 1 bonnet and 3 socks mysteriously lost, 1 fall,
74 doors knocked on, 1 memorable meeting at the Waldorf Astoria, 2 rejections,
10 lost addresses, 412 smiles exchanged, 10,000 hours getting permission,
12 hamburgers, 4 knishes, 8 hot dogs, 24 falafels, 6 great restaurants,
210 cafés, 14 bottles of Coppola's Director's Cut Cinéma© wine,
1 shameful number of cupcakes, 2 cherished pecan pies, 45 liters of caffeinated,
sugar-free soda, 128 weekends working flat out, 1 case of jet lag overcome,
32 mechanical pencils, 6 rubbers, 5 energy-efficient light bulbs,
1 new pair of glasses, 300 more hours getting permission, 48 nights on a sofa,
2 tubes of Voltarene©, 110,000 characters of text written, 72 friends to call back,
3 birthdays cut short, 0 temper tantrums or sulking,
and above all 100 billion giggles and unforgettable memories leading
to this new volume that we are thrilled to bring you.

CREDITS

• **PAGE 10** *YOU'VE GOT MAIL*. 1998. Director: Nora Ephron. Screenwriters: Nora Ephron, Delia Ephron. Producers: Nora Ephron, Lauren Shuler Donner. Associate Producer: Dianne Dreyer. Co-producer: Donald J. Lee Jr. • **PAGE 12** *MANHATTAN*. 1979. Director: Woody Allen. Screenwriters: Woody Allen, Marshall Brickman. Executive Producers: Robert Greenhut, Jack Rollins. Producer: Charles H. Joffe. • **PAGE 14** *BLACK SWAN*. 2010. Director: Darren Aronofsky. Screenwriters: Mark Heyman, Andres Heinz, John J. McLaughlin. Adapted from the Andres Heinz's novel. Producers: Arnie Messer, Mike Medavoy, Scott Franklin, Brian Oliver. Co-producers: Jerry Fruchtman, Joseph P. Reidy. • **PAGE 16** *ROSEMARY'S BABY*. 1968. Director: Roman Polanski. Screenwriter: Roman Polanski. Adapted from Ira Levin's novel. Producer: William Castle. Associate Producer: Dona Holloway. • **PAGE 18** *NIGHT AT THE MUSEUM*. 2006. Director: Shawn Levy. Screenwriters: Robert Ben Garant, Thomas Lennon. Adapted from Milan Trenc's novel. Executive Producers: Thomas M. Hammel, Ira Shuman, Mark Radcliffe. Producers: Shawn Levy, Michael Barnathan, Chris Columbus. • **PAGE 20** *2 DAYS IN NEW YORK*. 2012. Director: Julie Delpy. Screenwriters: Julie Delpy, Alexia Landeau, Alexandre Nahon. Executive Producers: Theodore Au, Helge Sasse. Delegate Producers: Matthias Triebel, Christophe Mazodier. Producers: Scott Franklin, Julie Delpy, Ulf Israel, Hubert Toint, Jean-Jacques Neira. Associate Producers: Dominique Boutonnat, Arnaud Bertrand, Hubert Caillard, Gérald Frydman, Jean-Claude Fleury, David Claikens, Alex Verbaere. • **PAGE 22** *ENCHANTED*. 2007. Director: Kevin Lima. Screenwriter: Bill Kelly. Executive Producers: Christopher Chase, Sunil Perkash, Ezra Swerdlow. Producers: Barry Josephson, Barry Sonnenfeld. • **PAGE 24** *MADAGASCAR*. 2005. Directors: Eric Darnell, Tom McGrath. Screenwriters: Mark Burton, Billy Frolick, Eric Darnell, Tom McGrath. Producers: Teresa Cheng, Mireille Soria. • **PAGE 26** *LOVE STORY*. 1970. Director: Arthur Hiller. Screenwriter: Erich Segal. Producer: Howard G. Minsky. • **PAGE 28** *SERENDIPITY*. 2001. Director: Peter Chelsom. Screenwriter: Marc Klein. Producers: Simon Fields, Peter Abrams, Robert L. Levy. Delegate Producers: Bob Osher, Julie Goldstein, Amy Slotnick. • **PAGE 30** *LÉON THE PROFESSIONAL*. 1994. Director: Luc Besson. Screenwriter: Luc Besson. Executive Producer: Claude Besson. Co-producer: Luc Besson. Delegate Producer: Bernard Grenet. Producer: Patrice Ledoux. • **PAGE 32** *KRAMER VS. KRAMER*. 1979. Director: Robert Benton. Screenwriter: Robert Benton. Adapted from Avery Corman's novel. Producers: Richard Fischoff, Stanley R. Jaffe. Associate Producer: Richard Fischoff. • **PAGE 34** *W.E*. 2011. Director: Madonna. Screenwriters: Madonna, Alek Keshishian. Executive Producers: Scott Franklin, Donna Gigliotti. Producers: Madonna, Kris Thykier. Co-producers: Colin Vaines, Sara Zambreno. Delegate Producer: Harvey Weinstein. • **PAGE 36** *THREE DAYS OF THE CONDOR*. 1975. Director: Sydney Pollack. Screenwriters: Lorenzo Semple Jr., David Rayfield. Adapted from James Grady's novel. Producer: Stanley Schneider. Delegate Producer: Dino De Laurentiis. • **PAGE 40** *THE GREAT GATSBY*. 2013. Director: Baz Luhrmann. Screenwriters: Craig Pearce, Baz Luhrmann. Adapted from the F. Scott Fitzgerald's novel. Producers: Baz Luhrmann, Lucy Fisher, Catherine Martin, Douglas Wick. Delegate Producers: Jay-Z, Barrie M. Osborne. Co-producer: Anton Monsted. • **PAGE 42** *BIG*. 1988. Director: Penny Marshall. Screenwriters: Gary Ross, Anne Spielberg. Producers: James L. Brooks, Robert Greenhut. Co-producers: Gary Ross, Anne Spielberg. • **PAGE 44** *BREAKFAST AT TIFFANY'S*. 1961. Director: Blake Edwards. Screenwriter: George Axelrod. Adapted from Truman Capote's novel. Producers: Martin Jurow, Richard Shepherd. • **PAGE 46** *TAXI DRIVER*. 1976. Director: Martin Scorsese. Screenwriter: Paul Schrader. Producers: Julia Phillips, Michael Phillips. Associate Producer: Phillip M. Goldfarb. • **PAGE 47** *THE SEVEN YEAR ITCH*. 1955. Director: Billy Wilder. Screenwriters: Billy Wilder,

George Axelrod. Adapted from George Axelrod's novel. Producers: Charles K. Feldman, Billy Wilder. Associate Producer: Doane Harrison. • **PAGE 48** *WEEK-END AT THE WALDORF*. 1945. Director: Robert Z. Leonard. Screenwriters: Sam Spewack, Bella Spewack, Guy Bolton. Adapted from the Vicki Baum's novel. Producers: Arthur Hornblow Jr, Robert Z. Leonard. • **PAGE 50** *MAN ON A LEDGE*. 2012. Director: Asger Leth. Screenwriter: Pablo F. Fenjves. Executive Producers: David Ready, Jake Myers. Producers: Lorenzo di Bonaventura, Mark Vahradian. • **PAGE 52** *REVOLUTIONARY ROAD*. 2008. Director: Sam Mendes. Screenwriter: Justin Haythe. Adapted from Richard Yates's novel. Executive Producers: David Thompson, Henry Fernaine, Marion Rosenberg. Producers: John N. Hart, Scott Rudin, Bobby Cohen, Sam Mendes. • **PAGE 54** *THE AVENGERS*. 2012. Director: Joss Whedon. Screenwriters: Joss Whedon, Zak Penn. Adapted from Stan Lee and Jack Kirby's novel. Producer: Kevin Feige. Delegate Producers: Alan Fine, Stan Lee, Jon Favreau, Louis D'Esposito, Patricia Whitcher, Victoria Alonso, Jeremy Latcham. • **PAGE 56** *THE DAY AFTER TOMORROW*. 2004. Director: Roland Emmerich. Screenwriters: Roland Emmerich, Jeffrey Nachmanoff. Executive Producer: Stephanie Germain. Producers: Mark Gordon (II), Roland Emmerich Co-producer: Callum Greene. • **PAGE 58** *THE MUPPETS TAKE MANHATTAN*. 1984. Director: Frank Oz. Screenwriters: Frank Oz, Tom Patchett, Jay Tarses. Adapted from Jay Tarses and Tom Patchett's novel. Executive Producer: Jim Henson. Producer: David Lazer. • **PAGE 62** *THE GODFATHER*. 1972. Director: Francis Ford Coppola. Screenwriters: Francis Ford Coppola, Mario Puzo. Adapted from Mario Puzo's novel. Producers: Albert S. Ruddy. • **PAGE 64** *NEW YEAR'S EVE*. 2011. Director: Garry Marshall. Screenwriter: Katherine Fugate. Executive Producer: Diana Pokorny. Producers: Mike Karz, Wayne Rice, Richard Brener, Toby Emmerich. Co-producer: Diana Pokorny. Delegate Producer: Heather Hall. • **PAGE 66** *WALL STREET*. 1987. Director: Oliver Stone. Screenwriters: Oliver Stone, Stanley Weiser. Producer: Edward R. Pressman. Co-producer: A.Kitman Ho. Associate producer: Michael Flynn • **PAGE 68** *BROADWAY DANNY ROSE*. 1984. Director: Woody Allen. Screenwriter: Woody Allen. Executive Producer: Charles H. Joffe. Producer: Robert Greenhut. Associate Producer: Michael Peyser. • **PAGE 69** *TOOTSIE*. 1982. Director: Sydney Pollack. Screenwriters: Larry Gelbart, Barry Levinson, Elaine May, Murray Schisgal, Robert Garland, Don McGuire. Adapted from Don McGuire and Larry Gelbart's novel. Executive Producer: Charles Evans (II). Producers: Sydney Pollack, Dick Richards, Ronald L. Schwarzy. • **PAGE 72** *THE OTHER GUYS*. 2010. Director: Adam McKay. Screenwriters: Chris Henchy, Adam McKay. Producers: Will Ferrell, Adam McKay, Patrick Crowley, Jimmy Miller. Co-producers: Jessica Elbaum, Joshua Church. Associate Producer: William M. Connor. • **PAGE 74** *SIDE EFFECTS*. 2013. Director: Steven Soderbergh. Screenwriter: Scott Z. Burns. Executive Producers: Douglas Hansen, James D. Stern, Michael Polaire. Producers: Scott Z. Burns, Lorenzo di Bonaventura, Gregory Jacobs. Co-producers: Elena de Leonardis, Sasha Bardey. • **PAGE 76** *GOING THE DISTANCE*. 2010. Director: Nanette Burstein. Screenwriter: Geoff LaTulippe. Producers: Adam Shankman, Jennifer Gibgot, Garrett Grant. • **PAGE 78** *NINE ½ WEEKS*. 1986. Director: Adrian Lyne. Screenwriters: Sarah Kernochan, Patricia Louisianna Knop. Executive Producers: Keith Barish, Frank Konigsberg. Producers: Antony Rufus Isaacs, Sidney Kimmel, Zalman King. Associate Producers: Steven Reuther, Stephen J. Ross. • **PAGE 80** *KING KONG*. 1933. Directors: Ernest B. Schœdsack, Merian C. Cooper. Screenwriters: Ruth Rose, James Ashmore Creelman. Producers: Ernest B. Schœdsack, Merian C. Cooper. Executive Producer: David O. Selznick. • **PAGE 84** *SLEEPERS*. 1996. Director: Barry Levinson. Screenwriters: Barry Levinson, Lorenzo Carcaterra. Adapted from Lorenzo Carcaterra's novel. Executive Producer: Peter Giuliano. Producers: Steve Golin,

Barry Levinson. Co-producer: Lorenzo Carcaterra. Associate Producer: Gerrit van der Meer. • **PAGE 86** *INSIDE LLEWYN DAVIS*. 2013. Directors: Ethan Coen, Joel Coen. Screenwriters: Ethan Coen, Joel Coen. Producers: Ethan Coen, Joel Coen, Scott Rudin. Delegate Producers: Robert Graf, Olivier Courson, Ron Halpern. • **PAGE 90** *SPIDER-MAN 2*. 2004. Director: Sam Raimi. Screenwriters: David Koepp, Alfred Gough, Miles Millar, Michael Chabon, Alvin Sargent. Executive Producers: Stan Lee, Joseph M. Caracciolo, Kevin Feige. Producers: Laura Ziskin, Avi Arad, Lorne Orleans. Co-producer: Grant Curtis. • **PAGE 92** *RAGING BULL*. 1980. Director: Martin Scorsese. Screenwriters: Paul Schrader, Mardik Martin. Adapted from Jake La Motta's novel. Producers: Robert Chartoff, Irwin Winkler. Associate Producers: Hal W. Polaire, Peter Savage. • **PAGE 96** *MICHAEL CLAYTON*. 2007. Director: Tony Gilroy. Screenwriter: Tony Gilroy. Executive Producers: George Clooney, Anthony Minghella, James Holt, Steven Soderbergh. Producers: Jennifer Fox, Christopher Goode, Kerry Orent, Steve Samuels, Sydney Pollack. • **PAGE 98** *THE DEVIL WEARS PRADA*. 2006. Director: David Frankel. Screenwriter: Aline Brosh McKenna. Adapted from Lauren Weisberger's novel. Executive Producers: Joseph M. Caracciolo Jr., Carla Hacken, Karen Rosenfelt. Producer: Wendy Finerman. • **PAGE 100** *GHOSTBUSTERS*. 1984. Director: Ivan Reitman. Screenwriters: Harold Ramis, Dan Aykroyd. Executive Producer: Bernie Brillstein. Producer: Ivan Reitman. Associate Producers: Joe Medjuck, Michael C. Gross. • **PAGE 102** *NEW YORK, I LOVE YOU*. 2008. Director: Jiang Wen. Screenwriters: Hu Hong, Yao Meng, Israel Horovitz. Executive Producers: Susanne Bohnet, Rose Ganguzza, Pamela Hirsch, Taylor Kephart, Jan Körbelin, Celine Rattray, Bradford W. Smith, Steffen Aumueller, Glenn M. Stewart, Marianne Maddalena, Claus Clausen. Producers: Emmanuel Benbihy, Marina Grasic, Marianne Maddalena. Co-producer: Bennett Parker C. Associate Producers: Pierre Asseo, Laurent Constanty, Warren T. Goz, Stewart McMichael. • **PAGE 104** *LAST NIGHT*. 2010. Director: Massy Tadjedin. Screenwriter: Massy Tadjedin. Producers: Christophe Riandée, Massy Tadjedin, Nick Wechsler. • **PAGE 106** *JULIE & JULIA*. 2009. Director: Nora Ephron. Screenwriter: Nora Ephron. Adapted from Julia Child, Alex Prud'homme, Julie Powell's novel. Producers: Laurence Mark, Eric Steel, Nora Ephron, Amy Robinson. Co-producer: Dianne Dreyer. Associate Producer: J.J. Sacha. • **PAGE 110** *HOLLYWOOD ENDING*. 2002. Director: Woody Allen. Screenwriter: Woody Allen. Executive Producer: Stephen Tenenbaum. Producer: Letty Aronson. Co-producer: Helen Robin. Delegate Co-producers: Charles H. Joffe, Jack Rollins. • **PAGE 112** *HITCH*. 2005. Director: Andy Tennant. Screenwriter: Kevin Bisch. Executive Producers: Wink Mordaunt, Michael Tadross. Producers: Will Smith, James Lassiter, Teddy Zee. • **PAGE 116** *NOUS YORK*. 2012. Directors: Géraldine Nakache, Hervé Mimran. Screenwriter: Isabelle Querrioux. Executive Producer: Farid Chaouche. Producers: Aïssa Djabri, Farid Lahouassa. Co-producer: Romain Le Grand. Associate Producer: Florian Genetet-Morel. • **PAGE 120** *FRIENDS WITH BENEFITS*. 2011. Director: Will Gluck. Screenwriters: Will Gluck, Keith Merryman, David A. Newman. Adapted from an idea of Harley Peyton, Keith Merryman, David A. Newman. Producers: Jerry Zucker, Liz Glotzer, Martin Shafer, Will Gluck, Janet Zucker. Co-producers: Nicolas Stern, Alicia Emmrich. • **PAGE 122** *WHATEVER WORKS*. 2009. Director: Woody Allen. Screenwriter: Woody Allen. Producers: Letty Aronson, Stephen Tenenbaum. Delegate Co-producers: Jack Rollins, Charles H. Joffe. • **PAGE 124** *WHEN HARRY MET SALLY*. 1989. Director: Rob Reiner. Screenwriter: Nora Ephron. Producers: Rob Reiner, Andrew Scheinman. Co-producers: Steve Nicolaides, Jeffrey Stott. Associate Producer: Nora Ephron. • **PAGE 126** *FRANCES HA*. 2012. Director: Noah Baumbach. Screenwriters: Noah Baumbach, Greta Gerwig. Producers: Noah Baumbach, Lila Yacoub, Scott Rudin. • **PAGE 128** *MORNING GLORY*. 2010. Director: Roger Michell.

Screenwriter: Aline Brosh McKenna. Production Design by: Mark Friedberg. Producers: Bryan Burk, J.J. Abrams. Associate Producers: Udi Nedivi, Lindsey Weber. • **PAGE 130** *CHINESE PUZZLE*. 2013. Director: Cédric Klapisch. Screenwriter: Cédric Klapisch. Executive Producer: Raphaël Benoliel. Producers: Bruno Levy, Cédric Klapisch. Co-producer: Buzz Koenig. • **PAGE 134** *I AM LEGEND*. 2007. Director: Francis Lawrence. Screenwriters: Akiva Goldsman, Mark Protosevich. Adapted from Richard Matheson's novel. Executive Producers: Michael Tadross, Dana Goldberg, Erwin Stoff, Bruce Berman. Producers: David Heyman, Akiva Goldsman, Neal H. Moritz, James Lassiter. Co-producers: Tracy Tormé, Jeffrey Wetzel. • **PAGE 136** *THE APRIL FOOLS*. 1969. Director: Stuart Rosenberg. Screenwriter: Hal Dresner. Producer: Gordon Carroll. • **PAGE 138** *TITANIC*. 1997. Director: James Cameron. Screenwriter: James Cameron. Executive Producer: Rae Sanchini. Producers: James Cameron, Jon Landau. Co-producers: Al Giddings, Grant Hill, Sharon Mann. Associate Producer: Pamela Easley • **PAGE 140** *THE IMMIGRANT*. 2013. Director: James Gray. Screenwriters: James Gray, Ric Menello. Executive Producers: Agnès Mentre, Vincent Maraval, Brahim Chioua, Molly Conners, Maria Cestone, Sarah Johnson Redlich, Hoyt David Morgan, Bruno Wu, Len Blavatnik, Jacob Pechenik. Producers: Anthony Katagas, Greg Shapiro, Christopher Woodrow, James Gray. • **PAGE 144** *ONCE UPON A TIME IN AMERICA*. 1984. Director: Sergio Leone. Screenwriters: Leonardo Benvenuti, Piero De Bernardi, Enrico Medioli, Franco Arcalli, Franco Ferrini, Sergio Leone. Adapted from Harry Grey's novel. Executive Producer: Claudio Mancini. Producer: Arnon Milchan. • **PAGE 146** *THE DEPARTED*. 2006. Director: Martin Scorsese. Screenwriter: William Monahan. Executive Producers: G. Mac Brown, Doug Davison, Roy Lee, Kristin Hahn. Producers: Brad Grey, Brad Pitt, Graham King, Gianni Nunnari. Co-producers: Joseph P. Reidy, Michael Aguilar, Rick Schwartz. Associate Producer: Emma Tillinger Koskoff. • **PAGE 148** *EAT PRAY LOVE*. 2010. Director: Ryan Murphy. Screenwriters: Jennifer Salt, Ryan Murphy. Adaptateur: Ryan Murphy. Adapted from Elizabeth Gilbert's novel. Executive Producers: Stan Wlodkowski, Jeremy Kleiner, Brad Pitt. Producer: Dede Gardner. • **PAGE 150** *SEX AND THE CITY*. 2008. Director: Michael Patrick King. Screenwriter: Michael Patrick King. Adapted from Candace Bushnell's novel. Executive Producer: Richard Brener. Producers: Darren Star, John P. Melfi, Sarah Jessica Parker, Eric M. Cyphers, Michael Patrick King. Associate Producer: Melinda Relyea, Delegate Producer: Jonathan Filley.

COPYRIGHTS PHOTOS

Original edition published in 2014 by Éditions du Chêne
© Éditions du Chêne – Hachette Livre, 2014
www.editionsduchene.fr

Authors: Barbara Boespflug and Beatrice Billon

Managing Editor: Flavie Gaidon
Assistant Editor: Françoise Mathay,
assisted by Camille Mansour and Marianne Toussaint
Translation from French: Bernard Wooding
Proofreading: Lyn Thompson Lemaire
Art Direction: Sabine Houplain,
assisted by Claire Mieyeville and Cassandre Esteve
Design and Layout: Baptiste Chazelle
Cover Design and Layout: Timothy Durand
Photoengraving: Quat'Coul
Production: Marion Lance
Partnerships and Direct Sales: Mathilde Barrois
(mbarrois@hachette-livre.fr)
Press Relations: Hélène Maurice
(hmaurice@hachette-livre.fr)

Published by Éditions du Chêne
(43, quai de Grenelle, 75905 Paris Cedex 15)
Printed in February 2014 by Estella Graficas in Spain
Copyright Registration: February 2014
ISBN 978-2-81230-986-1
32/3940/7-01